A Rocking-Horse Catholic

A
Rocking-Horse Catholic

Caryll Houselander

Christian Classics, Inc.
Westminster, Maryland
1988

First Published, 1960
Reprinted, 1988

Printed in the U.S.A.

A Rocking-Horse Catholic

Chapter 1

I was received into the Church when I was six years old. Strictly speaking, therefore, I am not a "cradle" Catholic but a "rocking-horse" Catholic.

At the time of my birth my parents, both of whom had been baptised into the Protestant Church, did not believe in or practise any definite religion at all; neither, I think, did they attach the least importance to any.

Nevertheless, two attempts were made to baptise me during the first few hours of my life. This was because my maternal uncle, a gynaecologist who had been called to his sister's bedside, and who was a conscientious though doubting and bewildered Protestant, habitually ordered immediate baptism for all babies in danger of death. He rightly considered this part of his duty as a doctor. As I was thought to be dying, my uncle sent for the nearest available Protestant clergyman to baptise me.

When the clergyman asked for my name, my mother and my uncle both had a fit of the giggles, the reason (so my uncle, from whom I have the story, told me) being that they had not thought it necessary to think of names for "something that would not live for twenty-four hours." Added to that, he said that I was so small and so odd, and so like a tiny red fish, that it seemed that I should either be drowned in the baptismal waters or swim away in them.

The clergyman was outraged by their irreverence, which only aggravated their—probably nervous—laughter, and they became hysterical. At this the good man refused to go on with the ceremony, despite the fact that my uncle spluttered out two names on the spur of the moment—Francis, his own name (he was acting as godfather), and Caryll, the name of a sailing yacht on which my mother had spent some of the months preceding my birth.

The clergyman swept out of the house, speechless with indignation, leaving me in my uncle's hands, held over the salad bowl which had been improvised as a font. Neither he nor my mother had been sufficiently under control to know whether the good man had or had not baptised me validly before he went. On that, my uncle (determined that I should not be swept straight into Limbo for all eternity) proceeded to baptise me himself,

4

whereupon I took a turn for the better and completed the joke by surviving, to live what has already been quite a long life.

Until I was about five years old my family lived in the old Roman city of Bath in Somerset. It was a very beautiful little city, ringed with hills, and always in the evening filled by the sound of melodious church bells. Bath was too old a city to grow older and seemed never to change with the times. I remember it as being almost wholly populated by old ladies whose standard of good manners was rigid and for me impossible, and clergymen who seemed anxious to live down to children's levels, and consequently embarrassed them acutely. I suppose that I must have spent more time with the servants than with my parents, for though I was very slow in learning to speak, when I did learn it was with a strong Somerset accent as well as the West Country drawl—box was "baax," S was Z, and so on.

Certainly my most vivid memories were of my nurse, who had the beautiful name of Rose Francis and who was, or anyway seemed to me to be, as beautiful as a rose, with bright pink cheeks, dark eyes and soft brown hair done in the curious fashion of the time around things called "puffs"—very light sort of frameworks that gave their wearers the appearance of having masses of hair that stood out from their heads like wings.

I do not think that Rose Francis had any religion. If she had, she certainly made no attempt to teach any to me, excepting grace after meals, and that could hardly be called religion as it was not explained to us *why* we were to thank God for our food, which, as both my sister and I were poor eaters and faddy, we did not appreciate. Rose Francis' real religion was good manners and the curious kind of snobbery peculiar to many of the servants of those days. The code of manners was based on what "little ladies" did or did not do, and even that was not wholly disinterested. "Little ladies," we were told, did not stir their porridge or blow on it; they did not drink from their saucer, swing on the garden gate, or speak to the postman! It was this last that revealed that Rose Francis was not wholly disinterested, for both she and I entertained a consuming passion for the postman, and my habit of swinging on the garden gate in order not to miss him whenever he came up the road was exceedingly annoying to my nurse, who hoped for a word with him. That, I am sure, was the real reason why he was included in the code of manners. Years later, after she had left us, Rose Francis married the postman.

My memories of our life at Bath are few and isolated. Among the most vivid and certainly the most lively of them is Bill Reynolds, his cottage and his pets.

Bill Reynolds was a very old man who had once been my grandfather's groom, and seemed to have a great affection for my father, and for my sister and me because we were his children. Our favourite afternoons were those, I suppose about once a week, when we went to call on him in his cottage. Everything there, including Bill himself, was like a picture in a brightly coloured, immensely detailed children's book.

Bill was a very old man; it used to seem to me that there could not be anyone in the world so old as he was. He was not, however, in the least decrepit; on the contrary, he was a vigorous, apple-cheeked and cherry-nosed old man, with long white hair that grew down to his shoulders and a long white beard that grew very nearly down to his waist. He had blue eyes like periwinkles and a tremendous, indeed a thunderous, laugh. When, years later, a Low Church Protestant cook tried to teach me something about God, she showed me pictures of Him appearing through blue gaps in clouds like cotton wool, which were exactly like Bill Reynolds, except for the clothing and the nose. For whereas God wore a white robe and a kind of red scarf, old Bill Reynolds wore riding breeches and gaiters and a green corduroy velvet coat which was very beautiful because it was so old, and had not only worn to the shape of the magnificent, broad-shouldered old man but had been mellowed by many, many summers and taken the beautiful, varied greens of many suns. It was a coat that seemed to live.

There was also a Mrs. Reynolds, small, grey-haired, with a bun at the back of her head and eyes as merry as Bill's. She always made us feel welcome, but very seldom spoke; she moved about the kitchen baking scones and other goodies like a pixie, and never let us go without a packet of them to take away. But the most enchanting thing of all about Bill Reynolds was his pets; they filled the house, the garden and the stable. In the kitchen there were the cosiest cats I have ever seen, cats that looked like and purred like round black kettles, and because, like everything in the Reynolds' cottage, they were clean and glowing, they shone like polished kettles too.

But even more fascinating than the cats was the parrot, with whom they were very friendly, and who often rode about the cottage on the broad back of one or the other of them, and tried in vain to teach them its own not very refined vocabulary. It was a very old parrot; Bill used to say that it was more than a hundred years old, and that he was too. I think in the case of the parrot it was probably true, and perhaps very nearly true in the case of Bill.

Outside in the little garden there were rabbits in hutches, a tortoise, and in a small stable a very old, very fat pony, kept only as a pet as it was too old to work: it was a very happy pet, though, and drank beer by the bucketful and ate lumps of sugar soaked in whiskey!

It was undoubtedly Bill Reynolds who partly reconciled me to our Protestant cook's God a few years later —not that I thought God was as nice as Bill, but He was sufficiently like him to be interesting: at least, He was in the picture book, though less so in the cook's descriptions of Him, which showed Him as almost only a God of wrath with particularly angry reactions to little girls.

Happily, when we left Bath, Bill Reynolds, his wife and all his pets were still alive and still hale and hearty.

Consequently I kept a memory of him for many years in which he and his odd family seemed to be immortal. Even now, I can hardly believe that if I went back to Bath and climbed the little terraced hill to his cottage, I should not find Bill Reynolds there still, with his little pixie wife, his cats and his fat pony; Bill Reynolds, who was the genius of the old grey city ringed with hills and rocked with bells.

Another vivid memory of the days when we lived in Bath is of going on at least one occasion to my father's rose garden. I may have gone more than once, but only one isolated occasion stands out.

The rose garden was not attached to our house, which, like almost every house, was on a hill and had a garden that was really no more than several banks covered in ferns and converging in miniature green valleys. It was ideal for children to play in and had its own magic, but my father's rose garden was something apart, something enchanted and mysterious and unimaginably beautiful.

It was a long way from our house and walled by those high grey stone walls that are peculiar to Somerset and Gloucestershire. You came into it by a low and narrow wooden door, let into one of the walls. When, years later, I heard of the Kingdom of Heaven I imagined one must enter it, if at all, by just such a door, a door just high enough for a child to go through, and a man if he bowed low or went in on his knees—a very low, narrow door made from the wood of the Cross.

Behind that little door there was nothing in that

garden but roses: it seemed to me, as a very tiny child, to be miles and miles of roses, and even a roof of roses above my head, through which, when I looked up, I could see tiny patches of blue sky, glimpsed through their red and gold and white and countless shades of cream and orange and pink of a world entirely filled with roses.

When I was a child I do not think child psychology was taken seriously, or so popularly known as it is today, and it was thought quite in order to frighten children, not only as a means either of enforcing authority over them or punishing them, but even for the amusement of the grown-up person who did it. There were few men who, like Bill Reynolds, were kind to cats; even dogs were *thrashed* into obedience almost invariably, and a study of the so-called "comic" papers of the time reveals how the most appalling cruelty was considered amusing. One of the commonest jokes was to frighten a child, especially by something uncanny. So far as this was concerned, we were more than happy in our nurse Rose Francis, who seemed to be far in advance of her generation, and who never used fear either to exert her authority or to amuse herself, or—as I have sometimes suspected that our other servants did—as an outlet for her own superstitions and terrors. Today, no matter what criticisms we may make of the modern theories of child psychology and their possibly exaggerated views of the impressionability of childhood, we may be thankful that little children are *not* ruled by fear (and possibly the projected fears of adults) as they were when I was very young.

Once a week our nurse went out, and we were taken for our walk—or, in my case more accurately, pram ride—by one of the other servants, the cook or the housemaid. We always went by the same route, which took us past what seemed to me to be an *enormous* drain-pipe. There was a huge yawning hole into it, at the side of the road. Where and how it was attached to a drain I cannot imagine, and the story that the servants told us was that it was the home of Mr. Tayler!

Who was Mr. Tayler? He was the worst imaginable bogey, liable to rush out from his drain-pipe home and gobble you up, even on the very rare occasions when you had *not* been naughty; on those when you had, his hunger and his ferocity were insatiable!

We usually had to pass Mr. Tayler's lair on the daily walks that our nurse took us for, and I at all events passed in fear and trembling; but with the secretiveness which I believe to be very usual in small children concerning their inmost fears and feelings, I never spoke to Rose Francis of Mr. Tayler. Had I done so I have little doubt she would have laughed him to scorn, perhaps even have laughed him out of my consciousness.

Chapter 2

My memories of the time I am writing about—that is, the time when I was between two and four years old —are very hazy. They are simply isolated points that stand out and must have made and left a deep impression on me, for, though I cannot be sure today of their exact order and content, I can remember them as separate incidents. I can remember them as such vividly, and even, looking back over the years, I can see a fairly obvious connection between them and what was to happen later in my own soul. It is only those things in which I can see that significance which I have chosen to describe.

When I was, I think, about two years old, my sister,

who would then have been four years old, became seriously ill with tuberculosis. (Strangely enough, I have hardly any recollection of her before that time.) It was decided to send her to a nursing home in Margate, and as far as I can remember my parents went with her to take her there. She was then on her back in a spinal chair and wheeled in it to the train, while Rose Francis and I went with piles of luggage packed in trunks in another compartment. We were not going to the nursing home, though I suppose our nurse must have gone there to help settle the little invalid—but it so happened that nurse had a sister living at Margate, and with her she and I were to spend the night.

I remember that when we arrived at the station there was a high wind blowing, and I, an exceedingly tiny child, was obliged to run; indeed, I was almost being blown along the platform, and had an odd, exhilarating sensation of flying, which has been repeated in my dreams over and over again throughout my life. A kindly porter, thinking, I suppose, that I would be blown onto the railway lines, or lost among the crowds on the platform, picked me up and set me on the top of our huge pile of luggage. However, I was blown off it, and this time seemed really to be flying through the air, though evidently I landed safely on my feet and was not hurt.

But the important memory of our visit to Margate was not the station platform and the wind blowing from the sea, but Connie. Connie was the little girl of my nurse's sister with whom we spent the night. It is impossible to describe the effect that she had on me; it was, I think, my first experience, if not of objective and self-less love, at all events of objective and selfless admiration. In after years I conceived a real love for my nurse, and when she left us I was brokenhearted, but as a very small child I was wholly centred on myself and my own needs. I took my parents for granted, and my nurse was simply warmth, sugar biscuits, hot milk and safety to me. Connie was the first human being outside myself to whom my heart flew out. She was about my own size and wore a blue cashmere frock which, as was usual for baby girls in those days, came down to her feet. Her hair, which was yellow and like the down on a chicken, was cut short like a boy's, and she had white button boots on her tiny feet.

We were both supplied by nurse's sister with a tin mug and a spoon, and I, copying Connie, walked round and round and round under the big kitchen table, rattling the spoon in the mug.

It is difficult to describe the joy of that occasion. From where we stumped round under the table I could see the feet of Rose Francis and her sister pushed into cosy bedroom slippers and stretched out in front of a glowing fire in the kitchen range: I could see the bottom of their big white aprons, and their balls of wool (for they were evidently knitting) rolling down onto the floor from their laps from time to time, to be chased by a kitten who was playing in the hearth. But the superb thing was Connie herself, her fluff of canary hair, her sky-blue dress, her white boots, her odd staggering yet rhythmic gait, and the sound of the spoon rattling in her tin cup.

I think that was the one and only time that I ever saw Connie, but I have never forgotten her, and the odd piercing joy of my first conscious awareness of what was, to me at all events, the sheer loveliness of another human being.

I have only one other memory of Margate; that was a visit that I paid to my sister in the nursing home. She must have been convalescent then, as she was running about and playing with other children, though when she went there she was flat on her back in a spinal chair. A long time must have passed, too, because I had completely forgotten her and did not recognise her.

The matron of the home took me out to a lawn where the convalescent children were playing and asked me if I could pick out my sister from among them. I hesitated, confused and ashamed because I did not know her, the more so because our home was full of photographs of her, many of them huge enlargements. In those she was a plump, radiantly pretty little girl, with thick loose curls all over her head. There was no little girl like that here. Her hair had been cropped short like a boy's, and she was painfully thin. She was wearing a zebra-striped jersey, and seeing my confusion and hesitation the matron said, "Look—that is your sister, the little zebra!" and led me to her. I do not remember that she was pleased to see me, and I think it probable that she regretted leaving the other children.

However, I regained my own pride in her and was assured that one day her curls would grow again (which they did not).

From that time until she came home, I told everyone, "I have a sister, she is a little zebra," and suffered acutely but dumbly, not understanding when everyone laughed.

Chapter 3

I do not remember when we left Bath, the old grey city of bells and steeples, to live in Brighton. I suppose that I must have been between five and six years old, and my sister, who was back in the family again, seven or eight.

When I was six, I was baptised for the third time, so to speak—this time conditionally, in the Catholic church of the Sacred Heart at Brighton. It was the feast of Our Lady of Mount Carmel. I do not think that my mother was received into the Church at this time herself. Certainly it was not until several years later that she began to take me and my sister to Mass, and to force multitudinous prayers, devotions and pious practices upon us.

What, then, persuaded her to have her two children made Catholics? In the first place the influence of a family friend, George Spencer Bower, K.C., whom we children called, and whom I will call here, "Smoky." Secondly, the example of Catholicism given by a doctor who attended our family at that time in Brighton.

Dr. Paley was the son of a distinguished classical scholar who, influenced by Newman at the time of the Oxford Movement, sacrificed his career at Cambridge to become a Catholic. His son, our family doctor, certainly inherited the spirit of sacrifice and unworldliness. He was a man of great humility and reticence who, without a trace of ostentation, devoted himself to the service of the poor, and brought more than physical healing to *all* his patients. He had that rare and perfect charity which almost miraculously inspires confidence, gives strength and restores peace.

Smoky was an agnostic. He was also the most amazing and the most lovable person that I have ever known. He was not, however, loved by everyone; indeed, he made many enemies, for he suffered from violent nervous irritability, was disconcertingly outspoken and honest, and did not "suffer fools gladly." He made no bones about it that he was, and was proud to be, "high-brow." This did not mean that he sought the society of "intellectuals"; far from it, he loved simple, but intelligent, people, animals and children. So far as children were concerned, he did not love them indiscriminately: the pampered pet, the spoilt or silly child, was abhorrent to him; neither would he tolerate a whining or pert child; but one who was unaffected and unspoilt delighted him. He was one of those rare people capable of friendship with a child that is not spoilt by the least flavour of patronage.

He was, to his grief, childless himself, and it was surely a great grace for my sister and me that he attached himself deeply to us. Smoky longed to become a Catholic, but he was never able, as he put it himself, to "swallow the Faith." The Virgin Birth was his stumbling block. He just could not accept "the evidence" for it. He was a barrister used to cross-examining witnesses, and without the smallest intention of irreverence, let alone blasphemy, he used to say, "I am glad that I never had to cross-examine the Virgin Mary."

Besides being a fine lawyer and the author of many legal textbooks, Smoky was a great classical scholar, philosopher, student of Shakespeare, and, without being a writer of verse, a poet in his own right.

All the Law Vacations Smoky spent in our house in Brighton. It was he who, during those wonderful holidays, took us children for our walks or down to the beach, he who played cricket with us in our patch of garden, and above all he who read the most enchanting stories and poetry to us and taught us absorbing things about the history of mankind, in such a way that we did not know that we were being taught at all. I wish that I could convey the miracle of Smoky's personality, but I cannot.

There was one "game" that we played wherever we went. We would bring anything that we found on our walks or on the beach to Smoky, with the question, "What was this in the olden times?" Whatever we brought to him seemed to enable him to tell us almost "everything in the world."

To this day I remember bringing him a little pebble of glass frosted by the sea, a "sea jewel" I called it, and asking our usual question, "What was this in the olden times, Smoky?" He went back to the very beginning of the history of that chip of glass (enhanced, I expect, by his own vivid imagination): how it was first made, and then how, when it was a bottle, it may have been used at banquets long ago; the story, too, of the wine that was probably, almost certainly, poured into it; the vineyards and the people who made the wine; the countries where the grapes grew, warmed through with the sun, and the places, such as Rome, where perhaps the banquets were held. He, Smoky, told me that in the "olden days" glass was not clear, as it is now, and he spoke of a man called Paul—a "fiery man"—who spoke of "seeing through a glass darkly," and of another man, Jesus Christ, who at a "wonderful supper" almost certainly poured wine into a cup made of dark glass.

From this Smoky swept on to the building of ships, from the old wooden rowing boats with their galley slaves, to the magnificent Spanish galleons with their white and red and purple sails, like the wings of great birds straining for flight; and thence to the Spanish Armada.

He told then a thrilling story of storm and shipwreck, as full of beauty as of terror, and of how those proud ships went down and the bottles of wine taken aboard were broken in the raging seas—and then the continual action of the waves and the salt on the chips of glass through years and years and years—and the strange fantastic things at the bottom of the sea, with great ships passing over them.

Smoky did not hesitate, at this point, to throw in a few mermaids with long golden hair, which they combed continually, and voices of unimaginable beauty—he bade me find a shell and listen to their voices singing in it, amidst the murmur of the seven seas.

Finally he told us about the tides that gradually brought our sea jewel to shore, coloured by the blue and green of the waters and frosted by the glittering sea salt, and of the moon that drew those tides. The moon, for Smoky, was not just a globe of matter, she was a Spirit in veils of light, who drew the dark waters, scattering her silver radiance upon them, by the sheer magnetism of her own loveliness.

During the legal term I often spent weeks on end staying with Smoky in his house in St. John's Wood. Much as he detested spoilt children, he spoilt me outrageously.

My most vivid memories of these visits were of when I was about seven or eight years old, and had been a Catholic since I was six. (This is anticipating, but it seems to me to be so essential to give what I can of Smoky's personality that it seems justified. I shall have to go backwards to describe my rather odd reception into the Church; meantime you must meet Smoky, who was not only very largely responsible for my becoming a Catholic, but later for my remaining one.)

He was married to the daughter of an actor, the leading actor of his day, Sir Charles Wyndham. Wyndham was a stage name; his real name was Culverwell, and he was an American, in no way connected with the English Wyndham family.

Naturally Smoky's home was frequented by stage people, and the theatre was a central part of our lives. Rather to his wife's justifiable indignation, Smoky frequently took me to the theatre, at an age when I have no doubt that it was very bad for me. He used to take the royal box for the two of us, and we went to every sort of play, usually grown-up ones, far too sophisticated for me, and for that very reason all the more enjoyable. We went backstage in the intervals, which added to my excitement—and, curiously enough, did not detract from the reality of the play for me.

There were certain plays, however, that we went to, without going behind the scenes. One of these was *Peter Pan*—we went to it year after year, and driving home through Hyde Park, with the lights gleaming in the trees, Smoky would tell me that we were passing through the Never, Never Land, which I believed. I can remember lying awake night after night after seeing *Macbeth*, trembling and sweating with fear as I remembered the groans of old King Duncan, the fearful clattering of the daggers in Macbeth's hands and the ghastly little ghosts who rose from a kind of giant cauldron, in green limelight, during the banquet scene.

In spite of my nocturnal terrors, when Smoky came home from the Temple in the evening, I used to act scenes from *Macbeth* to him. I was a hideous child with a squint, but with rather remarkable long, thick, carrotty hair, which I suppose fitted me for the part of Lady Macbeth. I was particularly fond of playing the sleepwalking scene, but hindered from giving it the full dramatic force that I should have liked to do by Smoky's little dog, Spot, who, used to nothing but gentleness and welcome from Smoky and me, would look bewildered and startled at the words, "Out, damned Spot!"

Very often Smoky said to me, "If there is a Heaven, and if I ever go there, the very first thing that I shall ask God Almighty for will be an introduction to Shakespeare and to Socrates." Plato was in his blood, and he read much of his writing to me before I was nine years old; later, in my adolescence, he read nearly all of it to me.

Not content with teaching me to love the theatre, poetry and philosophy and to believe in God, angels and fairies, or reading poetry to me in English for the sense and the sound, and in Greek simply for the music, Smoky instructed me in the English law, telling me repeatedly that it was founded on the Ten Commandments, in the days before the Reformation undermined the Englishman's belief in them, and insisting upon justice as the basic and essential virtue for everyone. Sometimes as a great treat, and it *was* a great treat to me, he took me to the Law Courts to hear him plead a case. It was in the Law Courts that, seized with an ecstasy of admiration for Smoky, I wrote one of my first "poems." I still have the original copy, written in a child's almost illegible handwriting on a sheet torn out of Smoky's junior's notebook:

> Mr. Bower was seated down
> In the court in wig and gown.
> His face was hot and fiery red,
> With perspiration on his head.
> He was the finest in the Court,
> So our noble Judge Bray thought.
> Occasionally he had a joke,
> But wisely and bravely Bower spoke.
> The words he spoke went straight to the heart,
> And he won his case with skillful art.

Now I must go back to the time when I was received into the Church, a few months before my sixth birthday.

Both my sister and I were frequently ill and were attended by the Catholic doctor I have mentioned, Dr. Paley. A friendship grew between his family and ours, resulting in almost daily walks and teas in one another's homes. The Paley family consisted of three children, one girl at boarding school and two little boys who, like us, were of nursery age and who became our constant playmates. There is no doubt at all that my mother was impressed by the religious upbringing of these children and began to think that her own children should be given the chance to grow up with the security of some definite creed to help them through life.

It was to Smoky that she turned for advice, and he who convinced her that if Jesus Christ was really God, and if he founded a Church, it was absolutely certain that this Church was none other than the Roman Catholic Church. He examined the evidence for this with the searching methods of an experienced lawyer, convincing my mother of the integrity of the witnesses, the four evangelists. Only absolutely honest witnesses determined to give the facts, he said, would have recorded the words of Christ on the Cross, "My God, my God, why hast thou forsaken me?"—words which, Smoky used to say, could easily have "lost the cause" for the divinity of Christ. He stressed the importance of the fact that the same honest witnesses told the story of the Resurrection, and of the forty days on earth of the Risen Christ.

There were two other points which Smoky was fond of repeating (and all the arguments he put forward to my mother, he put to me years later in my adolescence). The first of these points was that unless the visible Church was divine, and was really protected by the Holy Ghost, it could not have survived all the corruption that had assailed it in the course of history, through its own members. He gave it as his opinion that the Church's survival, with the absolute purity of its doctrine, was the strongest argument that existed for the divinity of Christ.

His second favourite point was the beauty and the all-inclusiveness of Catholicism. He used to say that it was the only religion in the world that includes all that is beautiful and good in every other, and all the poetry that is innate in the human race.

Finally, he urged my mother to bring us up as Catholics, and convinced her of the absurdity of the old argument that people brought up in ignorance of every religion are free when they grow up to choose which one they like.

Before being received, I had hardly any instruction. I remember one visit from a priest and being made to learn the Apostles' Creed by heart. I was given a brief explanation of its "articles." The explanation puzzled and saddened me, especially as I was told that it was myself who had crucified Our Lord by my sins. However, I had the instinctive awareness of God common to all small children, and was ready to accept and believe in anything I was told whether I understood it or not.

My sister and I were given conditional baptism together, without godparents. I remember that I was too small to reach the top of the font, and so stood on a chair to recite the Creed and knelt on it when the water was poured over my head.

After this we were taken to the Catholic church now and then by the family's manservant, usually in the afternoon. The manservant, who sternly disapproved of

Catholicism, never came in but stood waiting at the door until we came out.

I can well remember the first of these Sunday afternoons at what I suppose was the catechism class in church—an occasion of terror to me. Hawk (the manservant, very well named) took us. He was as grim and silent on the way as one leading prisoners to execution. At the door of the church he told us to go in, and turned his back, as if even to face the door would contaminate him.

The priest in the pulpit told the story of the conversion of St. Paul. Now it happened that I was terrified of horses. My fear was not of falling off a horse myself, or of being kicked or bitten by one, but of seeing a horse fall and injure *itself*. Consequently, when the priest told us the story of St. Paul falling from his horse, I panicked—the fact that the Saint was taken up into the seventh heaven meant nothing at all to me, I was filled by the vision of the plunging horse, struggling on the ground, and I sprang from my seat and tried to rush out.

At the door of the church I was stopped by a venerable old canon, much revered by his parishioners and, I have no doubt, a very holy man; but, alas, he was grotesquely ugly. He had one glass eye which seemed to protrude and stare, and one real eye which both squinted and swivelled in a terrifying way. With the kindest intentions in the world the old man seized me in my flight and tried to reassure me. Too petrified to scream, I remained dumb and paralysed in his hands, like a cornered mouse whose heart is giving out from fear, until a few minutes later the other children poured out and I was released, to be rescued by Hawk, who led me home, expounding on the wickedness of the Catholic Church in general and of Catholic priests in particular.

I suppose that had we been left entirely to Hawk we would have become nervous wrecks, but we were saved by our dog Jock, a rough-haired terrier of extraordinary fidelity who frequently took us for walks. Unlike Hawk, he had no aversion to Roman Catholicism, and it was considered on the whole more diplomatic to send us to church in his care than in that of the bigoted Hawk. Jock did not stand for any nonsense and did not allow us to talk to people in the street, whether they were priests or laymen. He waited patiently by the church door until the first worshipper came out; after that he would wait no longer, but would come in and rush about among the congregation until he found us, his special charges, and took us home.

Jock also took us to school, a kindergarten for "the sons and daughters of Jewish gentlemen." How we managed to gain admittance to that school I cannot imagine. All the other pupils and all the teachers were Jewish. Personally I was very happy there, though I could never understand why, whenever we got up to Isaac, we went back to Adam: however, I decided that the headmistress—a dark, handsome, very aged Jewess, with short frizzled hair and black flashing eyes—herself knew nothing beyond Isaac.

Jock, who had no religious prejudice of any kind, took us to this school every day, waited outside until it was time for us to leave, then, moved by some inexplicable instinct, barked unceasingly until we came out. However, I only attended for one term, at the end of which I contracted pneumonia as the result of acting as a mouse in the Christmas play, wearing nothing but a little mouse suit made of sateen. After that we left for good.

There is only one more experience of Catholicism that I remember during the time we lived in Brighton and after the time we were received into the Church. This, far from being alarming, was my first experience of something gentle, devout and tender, the first experience *after* I was received into the Church which seemed to show me that Christ Our Lord was actually *given* to us, put into our hands, and that we, who had evidently hurt Him, could also comfort Him.

One afternoon when we had gone to tea with Dr. Paley's two little boys—children who were, of course, far better instructed in their religion than we were—the younger of the two boys accidentally dropped his little metal crucifix that hung by his bed. Quite without self-consciousness, he picked it up and kissed the feet, very devoutly, very gently, before he hung the crucifix on its hook again. I watched him with wonder and have remembered the incident all my life.

B

Chapter 4

About a year after I was received into the Church, our family moved to Clifton, Bristol. It must have been there that my mother became a Catholic herself, for soon after we went there she started what I can only call a persecution of piety. Not only was she one who never did anything by halves, she always overdid whatever she did at all, whether it was sport, until then her main interest, or, as it now became, religion.

Until now we children had had hardly any religious instruction at all; now I was taken by my mother once or twice to a convent, where I sat under an overwhelmingly tall and gaunt, raw-boned nun who tried, without success, to impress upon me the importance of "saving" my immortal soul. However, the convent was too far away, and after one or two visits we ceased to go there. My sister went as a day-girl to another convent, nearer to our house, while for the time being my own instructions lapsed. Not, however, the practice of religion. At about this time priests started to frequent our house, where, in spite of his continued unbelief in Catholicism, my father entertained them lavishly.

My mother insisted that we should have little "altars" in our bedrooms, and most of our pocket money had to be spent on the deplorable statues, flower vases, flowers, lamps and candles and candlesticks, as well as lace and linen cloths, to put on these altars. They became positive riots of the worst that repository art can produce, but repository art has never worried me as it does more sensitive Catholics, and at that time I considered it extremely beautiful.

I did not dislike the altars, but what I did dislike and secretly resent was the long prayers we were obliged to say kneeling in front of them, and above all those that we said on the evenings when priests came to dinner. There was one of them who always came to listen to our prayers. I felt that we were not really praying at all, but being made to show off to impress this particular priest, whom—probably because of my mother's attachment to him, and the constantly reiterated falsehood that "all children loved him"—I increasingly disliked. Usually after the forced prayers were said, and the grown-up people were safely shut away in the dining room downstairs, I got out of bed and said my own prayers, in my own words, beginning by an apology for having already said so much that I did not mean. Then it was that I used to feel that God, whom I did know to be everywhere, was also localised on my altar, a feeling no doubt produced by the huge shadow of the Sacred Heart statue thrown onto the wall by the crimson lamp burning in the darkness.

Not only had we long prayers at home, but we were now taken to a great many church services on Sundays, sometimes to nine o'clock Mass at the local church followed by a very long walk to the eleven o'clock High Mass at the church at the other end of the town, where the priest whom my mother favoured was stationed. Later in the day we were often taken to catechism at the local church, and sometimes to Benediction after that. Added to this we were sent to the presbytery on certain weekday mornings to be "instructed" and occasionally, in my case, when I had been particularly naughty, to be lectured by the priest.

Again the religious instruction fell short of the mark; it consisted solely of looking at the coloured pictures in an illustrated Bible, excepting when it was delegated to another priest, a jolly, curly-haired little Irishman, whom children *really* liked, and who passed the half-hour playing rough-and-tumble games with us and squirting us with soda water syphons; I think *that* priest is among the influences that have kept me in the Church today.

Outside of church services, my mother devoted herself, though only for a few feverish months, to church bazaars and other such activities, most of which we had to attend.

Our experience of Catholicism during those first months at Clifton, which I am sure was an unusual one for children, could easily have turned us against orthodox religion for ever, but soon something else was to happen to me which could have been still more likely to prove fatal but for what I regarded then, and still regard, as a miracle, though I readily admit that it is capable of more than one natural explanation. I think of it as the "miracle of my second Communion."

First it is necessary to describe how I made my first Communion, and my first Confession. I was between eight and nine years old and still had not received any sacrament but baptism, and frankly, if I had come to the age of reason, I did not use my reason where religion was concerned. So far as the things of the spirit went, I was guided, if at all, by intuition, and by a sense of mystery and the beauty of God which I believe to be innate in all normal children.

Two things happened suddenly which were to bring about a complete inward change in my life.

The first was that a beloved governess, who had been with us for some years, left: she was a simple and devout Protestant, from whom we had learnt nothing about our own faith, but she was very beautiful, very gentle and very loving to us. Suddenly she left us, and certainly she left me bereaved and seeking for someone to fill the emptiness of her loss.

Shortly after she had gone my mother, with a large party of her own relations, went abroad to make a long tour of Spain. During her absence my sister went as a boarder to the local convent, and I was left to the care of my father, who was out all day at his office, and the servants, who left me alone to do exactly as I pleased. My father was equally indulgent: he supplied me with ample pocket money, and told me to amuse myself in any way I chose.

I wandered about Bristol, read books in book-shops and sometimes bought them, and, strangely, after the overdose of church-going to which I had been subjected, I went again and again to church. I preferred to go when no service was in progress, simply to kneel in front of the tabernacle. I had been told, of course, that Christ is really present in the Sacred Host, but until now I had known scarcely any personal reaction to this fact. It may have been because of the loneliness I was feeling after the loss of our governess that I was now drawn to the tabernacle as if by a magnet. In the presence of the Blessed Sacrament I was no longer alone, and I knew it now with the absolute certainty of a conviction that comes not from outside, but from the depths of one's own soul. I was possessed now by a longing to make my first Communion.

It happened that at that time a mission was being given at our parish church, the pro-cathedral, Clifton, and now athirst for knowledge I decided to attend it. It was a full-blooded Redemptorist mission. The seasoned Catholic knows well what that means; nothing was left undone to produce the dramatic atmosphere calculated by the good Fathers to snatch the damned from the very gates of hell. There were the usual two missioners who preached in turn each night—the first and more impressive to put the fear of God and Satan into us, the other who followed him up to supply a little soothing balm in the form of the *love* of God, for those rather timid old ladies who formed most of the congregation, and who were surely not much given to mortal sin.

It was the first, the wrath-of-God preacher, by whom I was impressed. He was a gigantic man with a face like an eagle and snowy white hair. He would walk down the aisle with deliberate, heavy slowness in the way that a coffin bearer walks at a funeral, but whereas the footsteps of mutes are silent or shuffling, his were clearly audible in a measured tread that suggested the approach of doom.

Slowly he ascended the pulpit, to pause for what seemed an interminable time, leaning over the congregation in his flowing black habit, one large black crucifix in his belt, another and bigger one behind him in the pulpit, his arms outspread like an eagle's wings. All of us held our breath, while slowly his eyes travelled round the church, searching each face in turn, as if they could penetrate through the pious masks that concealed the awful state of the sinners' souls from other men. Then, when the tension was at its height, he would let go: "Perhaps there is someone in this church tonight who is in mortal sin—someone whose soul is *dead.*" The innocent ladies would exchange uneasy, suspicious glances, one or two young men would redden in the gathering dusk, and the sermon would proceed.

It happened that my first attendance at the mission coincided with its climax, this very sermon on the state of the soul in mortal sin. No doubt everything had been leading up to this; I arrived just in time for the full blast.

I can remember that sermon vividly and in detail to this day—the missioner's face, his gestures, his terrible pauses and silences, the dim lights in the church and the gathering dusk, the crucifix with its terribly white body and its terribly red painted blood, seeming to lean over the missioner's shoulder—a crucifix as unlike the reality of the Crucifixion as anything could be, yet to a child deeply moving and even beautiful, with its flowering of roses and snow.

The sermon described what is meant by mortal sin, beginning with a very fair and moderate exposition of the three conditions necessary to commit one. The preacher certainly made it seem quite a considerable feat to succeed in committing a mortal sin, though I am bound to say he did not represent it as quite the superman achievement that I have heard a Jesuit missioner make it.

This preliminary disposed of, he swept on, not without relish, to describe the condition of one who *has* succeeded in committing mortal sin. He drew a vivid word-picture of someone shut up in a dark room with a decomposing corpse. We were spared no detail; first the stench that led the unfortunate occupant of the room to think that all was not well, then the awful discovery of the body, through fumbling about in the darkness until he laid his hands upon it. Finally, when a tiny chink of grey light filtered into the room, the appalling sight that met his eyes—a sight which I will spare you, but of which I have forgotten no detail.

The shock of this sermon was accentuated for me by the fact that until this evening I had known nothing at all about the physical aspects of death. As a child of four I had seen, or thought I had seen, the "ghost" of a little child who had died; I did not know at the time that she was dead, but learned it later. Her "ghost" was even more radiant and lovely than she, a beautiful little Jewish child, had been in life; my idea of a dead person, influenced by that little "ghost," was of the spirit, liberated, joyful and lovely. About dead *bodies* I was almost completely ignorant.

Now I sat shivering with shock and fear, nearly unconscious of the second preacher who went up into the pulpit to soften the blow. I registered only that he said, "Confessions will be heard after the service." I would gladly have followed the other penitents then and there to make my first Confession but, knowing that this was forbidden to children unless they had had some preparation, I went home through the dark streets trembling, to learn when I got home that my mother was expected back from Spain on the following day.

Chapter 5

She arrived laden with gifts of the most distracting kind—castanets of pale, polished wood with red and yellow tassels; inlaid brooches and combs from Toledo; sweetmeats made with ground nuts, so sweet that they made your teeth ache, and countless photographs of the crowned, vested and jewelled statues of Mother and Child that she had seen in the Spanish cathedrals.

After a radiant half-hour of forgetfulness, I remembered the mission, and asked my mother if she could arrange for me to make my first Confession. She agreed to allow me to go to the mission, but only to the children's services in the afternoons, and she said that I must speak to the mission Father myself about my first

Confession. This was easy enough. He stood at the door as the children filed out. I had only to stand beside him and pull gently at his habit when the others were gone. But I was a morbidly shy child, and on this occasion frightened too.

There was no reason for my fear. The Eagle proved to be a Dove. When I had sobbed out my story to him, he sat down in the church, took me on his lap, dried my tears with his own handkerchief, a huge scarlet one with white spots, and did all that he could to dispel my fears and to reassure me. Having won my confidence, he arranged that I should visit him each morning until the mission ended, in order that he himself should prepare me for my first Confession.

At the end of these visits, to my delight, he said that I could not only make my first Confession, which he would hear himself on the last day of the mission, but I could make my first Communion too, which the parish priest would give me on the following day. This, however, was not to be.

I made my first Confession on the tenth of March, and on the following day woke up with a violent chill that resulted in a long illness. It was not until July that I made my first Communion, on the Feast of the Precious Blood. Even then, I was told that I could do so only on the condition that I went to the altar dressed like any other member of the congregation—not, as is usual, dressed as a little bride, not with a "special candle" or flowers, or any other outward sign of a feast day.

I accepted these conditions joyfully. Shortly afterwards I was confirmed, taking the name of Michael after the Archangel on whose feast day I was born.

Before I was able to go to my second Holy Communion I was again attacked by illness, this time an illness which made a deeper impression on my whole subsequent life than anything that has ever happened to me before or since. It occurred with astonishing suddenness. At one moment, in spite of being a little prig in embryo, in spite of the shock of the mission sermon from which I seemed to have recovered, I was a normal child, not much afflicted by conscience and usually naughty rather than good; but a moment later I was literally prostrated by what must surely have been an acute and violent neurosis, characterised by an unbearable sense of guilt.

I was walking upstairs, going (unwillingly) to wash my hands for tea, when without a moment's warning I became too weak to take another step. I sat down on the steps feeling as if all my life was flowing out of my heels, and my wrists were too weak, too fluid, to lift my hands. There, after the tea bell had rung repeatedly and vainly for me, I was found, and carried upstairs and put to bed, where I had to remain for the next three months.

The doctor failed to diagnose this strange illness; other doctors whom he called into consultation failed too. It would be presumption on my part, looking back over so many years, depending on memories of childhood, to attempt to diagnose it myself. Nevertheless the symptoms, so far as I remember them, point to a psychological illness, probably hysterical in origin.

Physically, the most distressing and persistent symptom was acute difficulty in breathing, a continual temperature and ever-increasing weakness. These, however, were nothing at all compared to the anguish of mind and spirit which completely submerged me, which I could not explain to anyone, and for which no one could give me the smallest relief.

My poor mother did her best to help me, but what she did could hardly have been worse. She had always tried to inculcate in her children the idea that they "ought to tell everything to Mummy," an idea which I had until then absolutely repudiated. There was no one in this world whom I had ever felt able to confide anything to, except Smoky; moreover, I had a not wholly unjustified suspicion that "confiding in Mummy" was simply putting one's head into the noose by giving away one's secret misdeeds, a folly which always resulted in the kind of lecture which made the very presence of "Mummy" embarrassing afterwards and built up an abnormal reserve which froze me into a block of ice.

Now, tormented by feelings of guilt which I could not analyse or understand, I felt compelled to confide to my mother that I had committed some terrible sins. She took this seriously and insisted upon my telling her what these sins were. This she called "helping me to make my confession": it resulted in my making a very bad—because false, garbled and fantastic—confession to *her* nearly every day. I was in fact suffering from acute anxiety and struggling to attach this to some concrete act of mine and so discharge it, but I was too young and too ignorant to know that, and so wished myself into imagining I had committed sins which I had not, or grossly exaggerated those which I really had committed, hoping that by confessing these I could rid myself of the burden of guilt.

My mother took these confessions very seriously. Had she been a better-instructed Catholic than she was, she would have known that the Church, so much wiser a Mother than herself, forbids *anyone* to coerce her children into confessing their sins outside the confessional. But apparently ignorant of this, my mother spent hours sitting on my bed listening to my "confessions" and exclaiming with horror at them. It seemed that it was not God whom I had offended but herself. The priest to whom she was so devoted was to come later in the day to hear the same tale of woe.

My poor mother would sigh deeply and exclaim in accents of bitter shame: "Oh dear, oh dear, *what* will Father So-and-So think, when you tell him that?"; or, "Oh, to think of *my* child telling Father So-and-So she has done *that*!"

In the afternoon, nearly every afternoon, the priest would come. At this time the tongues of pious scandalmongers were already wagging concerning the frequent visits this priest made to our house. No doubt they supposed that his already almost daily visits to me were only a cover for spending long hours with my mother, but they were wrong. He spent long hours with *me*, hearing and re-hearing my tortured confessions, and seldom joined my mother downstairs until my father came home from his office.

I should make it clear at this point that this priest died later from a disease which gradually affected his brain and which, no doubt, had already seeded itself in him. No really normal priest would ever have treated a child as he treated me. He did not express the disgust and horror which my mother seemed to expect him to, but he did allow me to confess not once only, but often twice in the same afternoon, each time questioning me minutely concerning everything that I said. No sooner had he given me absolution for the first confession than I would beg to be allowed to confess again, this time declaring that nothing that I had said the first time was true, and that though I did know that I had done *something* very wrong, I did not know what it was. No wonder the priest, who was a truly compassionate man, was bewildered. I think he was struggling to find the solution to my state of mind but felt completely baffled.

Everyone who has ever suffered from "scruples" knows something of this obsessive anxiety about Confession, an anxiety which in the case of a reasonable adult can always be cured by gaining a true understanding of the sacrament of penance, instead of clinging to a distorted one, and by looking away from the rags and

44

tatters of self to the love and the beauty of God. I must have learned that intuitively, for one day when my anguish had reached a point beyond human endurance, and my physical weakness was causing increasing alarm, I told the priest: "I do not want to go to Confession any more—I want to go to Holy Communion instead."

"What—without Confession first?"

"Yes. I *can't* tell you what is the matter, but God will know without being told."

At first my request was refused—the doctor seemed to think that to receive Holy Communion might snap my last thread of sanity. But he did forbid any more confessions.

"Tell your trouble to God," the priest suggested. "You know that God is present everywhere, turn to Him and tell Him."

But for me the actual presence of the Blessed Sacrament in the room meant the presence of God; it had become the only way in which I could realise it. "If I may not receive Holy Communion," I asked, "can you not bring the Blessed Sacrament here and show It to me?"

No, this too was refused.

Only when I became so weak that my life was thought to be in danger did they at last give way. I was given my second Holy Communion as Holy Viaticum.

It was in the evening, I think. The room was dark, and the flames of firelight dancing on the wall seemed almost to cause me pain when I opened my eyes. They were beautiful, and beauty falling on my tormented mind was like scalding water falling on an open wound. I no longer attempted to translate my torment as particular sins; I had realised in a dim, intuitive way that it was not something I had *done* that required forgiveness, but everything that I *was* that required to be miraculously transformed. It was of *myself* that I required to be healed, and that could only happen one way, by a union in which I would be quite lost in God; and *that* I knew could only happen in Holy Communion.

The grown-up people were talking in whispers by my bed, and slowly the meaning of what they were saying came through the darkness that was on my own mind. The priest was on his way to give me Holy Communion because they had "no right" to refuse this any longer, and now it could do "no harm."

Presently the priest came in and the other people left the room. But the priest did not ask me to confess, as for a moment I feared he would. Actually it would have been impossible, as though I was certainly able to think, I was scarcely able to speak. Instead of the Confession, he himself made an act of contrition aloud for me and gave me absolution. I suppose that even the child in me, which had certainly been obliterated, was already on the way back to take possession of my soul, for I can remember a certain impish glee in the fact that the priest, who had so often made me say the act of contrition, now had to say it for me, while I had nothing to worry about at all. If there were any distractions, they would be his! I knew too that the grown-ups thought that I would die, but that I was not going to, and this too pleased the impish side of my nature, much in the way that making an "April Fool" of an adult would have.

The priest, still alone with me, broke the little Communion Host into fragments and gave them to me, as my ordinary medicines were given to me, in sips of water. I was instantly at peace—as if I had simply woken from a long nightmare to the security and blessedness of a sunlit morning. For a moment I remained, propped a little on the pillows, lying with my eyes closed; and it seemed indeed that a gentle, golden radiance shone through my thin eyelids and suffused my whole being, as the warmth and light of the sun penetrates and suffuses the earth, quickening the seed to flower.

Then when I opened my eyes I saw that the golden light was from the candles burning on the little altar by my bed, and the firelight that now lit the whole room with dancing flames. But the beauty of fire and light no longer hurt me, I could respond to it, and this response to beauty and the joy of being wholly alive was my "thanksgiving."

I sat up. This seemed to alarm the priest, who told me to lie down again.

I said, "No, I am going to sit up."

"But you *can't* sit up!"

"I *am* sitting up. Please bring my toy soldiers on a tray."

"But you must lie down and make your thanksgiving!"
The priest seemed increasingly alarmed.

He went out of the room and called my mother. She
was even more alarmed than he, and I was exhorted to
say my prayers in case, if I did not, I started "worrying"
again.

"I shall never worry again."

In the end, the toy soldiers were brought to me, but
they were put on the altar by the bedside, and I went
to sleep.

On the following day Smoky arrived from London.
He was the only person who accepted the fact that a
miracle had occurred. "Damn it all," he said in my
hearing to the devout Catholics who were vying with
each other in their attempts to explain the miracle
away. "Damn it all, it takes an old agnostic like me to
believe in God!"

I was up and riding on a donkey over Durdham
Downs within ten days, but I was certainly not given
the misguided homage which is sometimes given to those
who claim to have been miraculously cured. Far from it.
The doctors now declared that there had probably been
nothing the matter with me at all. Certainly nothing
worse than hysteria. Other people suggested that it
might have been sheer cussedness, a wicked hoax on my
part, involving my parents in hideous worry and ex-
pense in order to force the whole of my small world to
concentrate on me. Whatever the explanation, I was
under a cloud and regarded from that time onwards

with open suspicion as a neurotic—functional neurosis being regarded in those days more as a form of perversity than as an illness.

However, that did not damp my spirits. Personally, at that time I did not doubt the miracle. I was restored to my childhood; my childhood as it was before, uncomplicated by any unreasonable or morbid sense of sin; and I was no longer lonely.

I have dwelt at such length on this incident for two reasons. The first is that it has made it impossible for *me* ever to doubt the Real Presence in the Blessed Sacrament, which does not mean that I am unaware of, or will not consider, several other obvious possible explanations of my "miracle." It made it impossible, too, for me to question, as I tried to do in later years, that Christ in the Blessed Sacrament is given into the keeping of the Roman Catholic Church, regardless of whether its hierarchy, its ministers and its members are individually good or bad, wise or foolish. I will return to this later.

My second reason for dwelling on the incident is that my childhood experience of anxiety neurosis has conditioned my attitude towards psychological suffering during my whole subsequent life. I know the terrible reality of it, which I think that no one who has not experienced it can. The experience left me acutely aware of psychological suffering in other people, even when I was still a child, and it is largely my experience of these people and their suffering that has confirmed my faith in *Christ in man,* which in a sense is what the Catholic

Church is. Also, combined with long study of this kind of suffering in others, my own experience has convinced me that the only real cure for it is the touch of God. Contact, resulting in union with God. I am not speaking of clearly pathological cases or cases of insanity, but of that mysterious torment which comes from within oneself, and which in spite of the vast mass of experimental psychiatric treatment that is being used today, still baffles the medical profession, and usually defeats it.

Many of the lives of the Saints strengthen this conviction. Again and again we read of Saints who suffered acute and critical psychological illness, who at one stage seemed doomed to become failures as human beings, incapable of happiness, incapable of living fully, yet who at the "touch of God" recovered completely, to live gloriously.

Everyone knows the story of the illness of St. Thérèse of Lisieux, which was cured by a smile from Our Lady, a smile which not only dispelled the terrors afflicting the child but changed her from a tortured, oversensitive, neurotic to a person of extraordinary emotional and mental balance. There is a parallel to her story in that of the little Polish boy who lived hundreds of years before her—St. Stanislaus Kostka, who was cured of a nervous breakdown when Our Lady appeared to him and put the Infant Christ into his arms. He recovered, to become one of the gayest and liveliest of Saints, rejoicing in all that is beautiful on earth as well as in Heaven, living to become the patron of youth, and to make himself beloved to youth for all time, by his *joie de vivre*.

There are many other Saints too, who might have been neurotic instead of being saints but for a moment when God came to them, and their complete surrender to Him when He came.

Certainly everyone who is cured of a neurosis does not become a saint (I did not, as you will learn), though everyone *could* do so, if all surrendered to God as the Saints did. But all the evidence we have points to the fact that only God, brought to the tormented soul, somehow, by someone, can permanently cure psychological suffering, and then only if the will of the sufferer responds to God.

The "cure" is not, therefore, confined to the chosen few who receive direct visitations from Heaven; it is available to everyone. Certainly God can choose to come to any particular man in whatever way He wishes, and in the case of those who are deprived of the Blessed Sacrament for any reason—such as inculpable ignorance, or being in circumstances that put them out of the reach of a priest—He can, if He does wish to, come in extraordinary ways.

One thing, however, is certain; when He comes, He will always come in the way that the particular soul can most easily realise and most easily respond to, and which is least likely to be confused with the possibility of hallucination. The ordinary way—and how amazing that it *is* the *ordinary* way—is in the Blessed Sacrament;

this is the way that even little children can realise, it is as simple to accept as the bread on the table, and it is the way that Christ Himself desires to come. That, surely, is one reason why He has given Himself to the Church, not only into the hands of Saints, but into the hands of all kinds of men, many of whom are sinners.

On the night before He died, when He instituted the Blessed Sacrament, He gave Himself for all time into the hands of Peter—and into the hands of Judas. A further reason why this way, the way of Communion with Christ in the Blessed Sacrament, is of such great value to those who are tortured by psychological suffering, is because it necessarily involves other human beings; someone must bring Christ to the sufferer, someone must *give* Christ to him. There are other ways, too, by which Christ has made Himself man's gift to man; the Mystical Body is planned for that. But this way, through sacramental Communion and the Sacred Host, is at the heart of the mystery of God's love, and from it flows every other communion and Christ-giving between men.

It is because the psychological sufferer is always cut off, isolated by his self-torment, from his fellow creatures, that this is so valuable to him. God must be brought to him by another man; only God can reach that centre of his soul that must be touched if he is to be made whole, but God chooses to come to him in Communion only if he will receive Him from the hands of a fellow man.

I have spoken of the "cures" of the Saints, because in them we can see what happens when the sufferer surrenders self to God wholly and immediately: the cure too is immediate—complete and lasting. Ordinary people who are not saints rarely surrender themselves so completely. It is likely to be a more gradual process; it may be only after many Communions that they will even begin to know God as He really is, well enough to dare to abandon themselves to and for Him.

The Saint, too, will not cease to make the *continual* offering of himself to God, but his offerings will have become like the offering up of a consecrated Host with which he has become identified, whilst those of the ordinary person will be like bringing the unconsecrated bread to the altar and putting the drop of water into the wine that is not yet consecrated.

Because these expressions, "surrender to God" and "abandonment," are so continually misunderstood, I want to define as clearly as I can what I mean by them here.

I do *not* mean, as some people have thought, *resignation* by "surrender"; I do not mean by "abandonment" that which, though it is often called "abandonment" to the will of God, is too often in fact abandonment to everything that is *not* the will of God. I certainly do not mean that the tormented soul should surrender his will to God's by accepting his suffering and making no further attempts to be rid of it; this would indeed be a travesty of "God's will," because this particular suffering consists almost wholly in obsession with self, and an obsession with self could never be God's will for anyone.

By surrender to God I mean giving oneself up to God, to be transformed in Him. It is the cure for self that is the core of the whole thing; we require to be cured of *self* by being changed, as the bread and wine on the altar are changed, into Christ.

In this surrender is, I believe, the cure for the torment of self, which is precisely what most psychological suffering is. It is the cure for the weakness that cannot carry the common burden of the world's sin; the cure for the fear that causes the will to wither before the challenge of life, the cure for the feebleness that makes the impact of natural beauty painful, the cure for the cowardice that causes the heart to contract and shrink before the challenge of love.

When a Saint surrenders himself wholly in this way, it is true that he will certainly accept whatever circumstances God allows for him. He may sometimes, because of his individual and unique vocation, go out to meet and welcome some of them. Such things as poverty, pain, bereavement, persecution—what you will—but he will not accept them or welcome them because he supposes them to be the essential things in his life, but because, compared to the joy, the power and the beauty of God, they will be almost nothing at all. They will be to him like leaves blown in the wind, the great wind of the Spirit of Love that sweeps the world like blown fire, setting it alight with His glory. For the Saint the surrender to God is a tremendous fling of the heart, comparable to a leap into the fire of eternal Love, to burn with its heat, to take the radiance of its light, to dance in the dancing of its flames.

For us it is a more secret thing, but none the less miraculous for that. It means that we begin to be able to *enjoy* life, and gradually gain in strength of spirit until we can *enjoy everything*. It is as secret and as real a thing as the change of the bread and wine on the altar to the Body and Blood of Christ; no one sees any change, no one sees anything happening at all, but it does, and what happens is a work of God, a work of God which is incomparable and happens over and over again, all over the world, every day.

So it is with us. If we offer ourselves, and let God transform us into Himself, we see the world with Christ's eyes, rejoice in it with His zest for life, love it with His Heart.

Chapter 6

One day after my ninth birthday, I came home from my donkey ride to receive a shock. Beatrice, our housemaid, was sobbing in the hall. Although few things are more frightening to a child than the sight of a grown-up person in tears, this would not have alarmed me in the ordinary way. Beatrice wept too often; she was a queer, overblown girl, inclined to melt into a kind of emotional soup and to develop a skin rash when submitted to the slightest strain. Today, however, the whole house was pervaded by an atmosphere of disaster. With obvious delight in imparting the bad news, between loud and strangling sobs, Beatrice told me that I had no longer father or mother or home; that, from this day on, I was no better off than an orphan in a foundling home—indeed, less well off, as no one in this world wanted me at all.

It is much to my parents' credit that, though they had long been bitterly estranged, they had never quarrelled in my presence; but the suddenness with which the blow struck me did nothing to soften it. My home—the house built on a rock, as I had supposed it to be—was to be swept away, and (as Beatrice took care to tell me) the reason was that my parents had quarrelled. My sister and I quarrelled very often, and it had always been impressed upon us that we must "make it up" before we went to sleep at night; to let the sun go down upon our anger was considered to be tempting Providence; one of us might die in her sleep, leaving the other to a lifetime of remorse! That grown-up people ever *did* quarrel was a new and shocking idea, but that, when they did, the quarrel could never be made up at all was something utterly beyond my understanding. It shattered my faith in grown-up people—most of all in fathers and mothers.

Emotionally children identify their parents with God. They stand for the things that the idea of God stands for to the human race as a whole—security, home, refuge, food and warmth and light, things taken for granted as unquestioningly as the love which provides them is taken for granted, and with the same innocent egoism of childhood. On the day that a young child learns that his trust in father and mother was misplaced, above all if one or the other has sacrificed him to some other love, emotionally if not consciously his trust in God is shattered. He will not, of course, reflect that circumstances may have overcome his parents; he looked to them for the invulnerability, the unchanging love that belongs only to God. This is why it is important to teach a child's mind as well as his heart. He *needs* dogma: the religion that consists of nice feelings, hymns and prayers at Mother's knee is simply a snare set for his feet.

The seeds of revolt against authority had been sown in me even before my home was broken. Now that attitude crystallised. It has complicated my life ever since.

Certain things that I *had* been told about God the Father and God the Son had led me to think, or at least to *feel*, that there was even enmity between them; for example, I was told that nothing could "satisfy" God for the sins of the world but the crucifixion of His only Son—an idea which represented the Father quite falsely as a monster of cruelty and injustice. No child, and no grown-up person, can understand the Blessed Trinity. But far too many children in the world are allowed to grow up believing that there is even antagonism between the Three Persons in one God. Father and Son are represented as having an endless feud, and the Holy Ghost as a rather ineffectual bird or a flaming tongue of light, introduced for no very clear reason.

It is not necessary to *understand* the Trinity in order to be convinced, and gladly so, that the whole relationship of the Three Persons in one God is simply unimaginable love. This should be the heart of all religious teaching. It is the essential thing to know—God's relationship to Himself. His relationship to men, incomprehensible though it is, flows out of this in wave upon wave of ineffable love. It is the essential thing to know, and it is easier for a little child to apprehend in his own limited way than anything else he can learn about his religion. It is the essence of religion, but it was not taught to me when I was a child.

In the boxroom at the top of our house I had built myself yet another altar. It was made from empty toothpaste tubes, twisted rather in the fashion of the curious beaded ornaments to be seen in French cemeteries. On it I had put a crude "holy card" of the Crucifixion which I thought extremely beautiful. Here I could hide myself and pray without an audience of mothers or priests, and my prayers consisted almost wholly of a child's pitiful attempts to comfort Christ for the monstrous cruelty and injustice (as I supposed) of the Crucifixion. It was to this secret altar that I took my disillusionment, and before it I vowed that I would harden my heart; from henceforth, I said to the crucified Christ, I would belong only to myself, I would go on my way locked in my own self-love. Brittle armour indeed, as brittle as the shell of a bird's egg, but it served me for the moment, perhaps because I was still so unhatched.

So it came about that in the January of the next year, as hard and sour as a green apple, eaten up with self-pity and in revolt against the whole world, I went with my sister to a little French convent in a suburb of Birmingham. I well remember the journey. We were to go to "Snow Hill," Birmingham, and there change for our tiny wayside station. All the way I longed to see "Snow Hill," for if I did not think it would actually be a hill of snow, I could not imagine that it would not be a place of extraordinary loveliness, white and glittering like a fairy story. When we arrived at what is surely among the greyest and dreariest stations in England, I knew the grief of disenchantment. But I was soon to be re-enchanted by a more lasting loveliness than any shining snow.

The convent was that one of which I speak in a rhythm, "The Parish First Communions," and again in "Soeur Marie Emilie."[1] It had the beauty of austerity, the wonderful shining cleanliness and even emptiness, the simplicity of having only what is essential, which is balm to the troubled mind. There was something for me that was almost sacramental in the substance of everything around us. It was as if God was laid upon us in the white linen sheets on our beds, and touched us in the touch of cold water. We seemed to breathe Him in the air that we breathed, and the morning light on the white curtains of the dormitory was His smile. Here I was made new and restored to the simplicity of my childhood before it had become complicated by suffer-

[1] Both published in *The Flowering Tree*.

ing and by feelings of guilt. It was as if my mind had
been washed by light.

> I am back again in the French convent
> and the austere, lovely morning,
> thrilled with the mute mystery
> of the day of the First Communions.

> The touch of cold water,
> the curtains round the beds,
> and the clean bare boards
> of the floor in the dormitory.

> I know that sin is something
> to be resisted strongly,
> with all my heart.
> I have the knowledge of innocence,
> learned by watching the flame
> in the pale-faced nun
> who taught me
> the lesson of sacrifice.

> She smells of lemon and soap and linen.
> Her smile is an inward smile,
> and her eyes of radiance
> teach the innocent heart,
> beating with austere joy,
> that sin is a terrible thing,
> redeemed by a passion of love.

The last cadence is literally true; the nuns, and this
"pale-faced nun" perhaps most of all, did not only teach

the love of God verbally, they showed it, they radiated it, some of them burnt with it. They were an amazing little community, intensely individual; one had everything here except mediocrity. All but two were French, and they had the vivid, irrepressible temperaments of French women. They were not at all even outwardly faultless, and sometimes, to our delight, quarrelled openly with each other in front of the children.

During the last war I was reminded of them by a little French refugee girl of twelve who mothered her five-year-old sister with adoring severity; when the baby displeased her she fixed, even paralysed, her with eyes that seemed to grow larger and larger and assume an incredible ferocity. This power of paralysing with a glare was possessed and used by several of our nuns; frequently on us and sometimes on one another. There were two who shared the charge of a big dormitory, and there was a feud between them. I have seen them standing facing each other, giving the glare, one small and rosy like an infuriated robin, the other scraggy and large like a spitting cat. It was told in delighted whispers among the children that they even put slop-pails in each other's way to trip each other up—but this may have been wishful thinking on the children's part.

I wish I could describe each nun in turn, for they were so varied, so different from each other, and they did and said such lovely, and funny, things, that if they were all told they would read like the *Fioretti*. But one thing they all had in common, from the rather enigmatic Mother Superior to the little gnome-like lay sister who loved and looked after the chickens and had really Franciscan power over them. The one thing they had in common was this, they never tried to serve God and Mammon.

I was to spend more time with the nuns than children usually do at school, because during the holidays that I spent there I lived with them almost as if I were a postulant, and I am quite certain that there was not one of them who was not poor in spirit—and poor in fact too. If the rooms *we* used were bare and austere, the community rooms—if their refectory and dormitory could be glorified by such a name—were poorer than any I have ever seen in a workhouse or a dosshouse. I think that the loveliness of the atmosphere in the school, its unique beauty of the sacramental quality in essential things, radiated from this spirit of poverty. Those nuns had emptied themselves of everything to possess the one essential for them—God: consequently, they did not only teach the love of God verbally, they showed it, they made it almost tangible.

The convent was a refuge for the children of broken marriages and unhappy homes. The Reverend Mother, a strange woman who was, I think, over-austere to herself and to adults, was possessed by a strong maternal instinct; she welcomed every tiny child dispossessed of its home and its own mother. She welcomed them, petted them, mothered them, and sometimes, I think, spoiled them. She received them at any age (the youngest in my day was three). Whatever there may have been to question in her treatment of them in the way of over-indulgence, she gave them the love essential to every baby child, and she gave them roots.

There were a great many rules in this school. One very wise one must, I think, have been insisted on as rigidly as it was to protect the children of divorced people, as well as to prevent snobbery; it was forbidden to speak of your family at all, or of how much or how little money your parents had, or to say what your father's business was. Of course this rule was constantly broken secretly, but it did much to teach the humility which was certainly one of the aims of the education that we were given.

This education was definitely French. Today I believe the school has grown, in a sense grown up; it has become more advanced, more English; more, I expect, the kind of school that most English girls like. Yet I feel sure it has not lost, and never will lose, that French spirit, with its mixture of logic and poetry and its genius for the love of God.

We were not, as in English schools, "put on our honour," a fact which added to the spice of life by a continual battle of wits between the children and the nuns, who were not ashamed to spy on us. Indeed, the school was as unlike an English public school as possible. Good manners, painting, music and embroidery were considered more important than games and "team spirit." Piety, far from being looked on as bad taste, was encouraged; even an open display of it was considered normal and "edifying." I never heard the word that I was to hear so often later in an English convent— "singular." Here, to be singular was not disapproved of; it was merely being yourself, and as such was encouraged.

Some of those who were at school with me have told me that they thought religion there was "overdone." Certainly we had it in full strength, with longer hours of prayer and meditation than I have known anywhere else, with long and minute examinations of conscience, and with daily catechism taught by the Mother Superior herself. We had to learn the catechism by heart of course, and on Sundays we had to learn the Gospel for the day by heart. We had spiritual reading for half of every mealtime, and it was nearly always the auto-biography of St. Thérèse of Lisieux in French, which most of us found quite sickening and seemed to dis-associate from the real devotion to her which we had. Her photographs were printed on the covers of all our exercise books.

In that convent there were really fasts, and feasts were really feasts. Lent was a serious business; we were taught to make countless little sacrifices, but taught too that to suffer with or for Christ was a supreme privilege. (If only every child learnt that early, how few people would carry psychological scars with them through life!) November, too, the month of the Holy Souls, was a time for many sacrifices, in which we were encouraged by an old nun who thrilled us by the most lurid and horrifying ghost stories, calculated to plant a total misconception of Purgatory in our minds.

But when the feasts came, what feasts they were! The feasts and the First Communions. I quote from the rhythm "The Parish First Communions" again, because those feast days cannot be described in sober prose:

> There is a smell of flowers
> filling the cloister.
> We are moving slowly in ranks.
> We are wearing long white veils
> and brides' dresses, down to our feet.
> The thin melodious singing
> is the singing of angels
> in the green paradise
> of children in love.
>
> Afterwards there is breakfast,
> the breakfast for feasts,
> with roses on the table,
> and the crimson may outside,
> and a bird whose singing
> fills my heart.
>
> I think my heart would break
> for joy of that bird singing
> right inside it,
> were it not that the nun
> restrains it with recollection,
> and we must have perfect manners
> and sit up straight at table.

There is a smell of coffee
and warm new rolls,
and each of us will have a banana
because of the feast.

I am back again in the French convent
and the austere, lovely morning,
thrilled with the mute mystery
of the day of the First Communions.

I enjoyed the holidays for many reasons. I had long
ceased to want to go home. Indeed the convent had become my home. I liked joining in the nuns' recreation,
though it is difficult to say why; I think that I would
find it exasperating today.

Although, as I have said, the nuns conformed to few
of the accepted conventions of religious orders, recreation was the exception; everyone, except the Reverend
Mother and two or three of the oldest nuns, was expected
to walk backwards very slowly—a more difficult business
than it sounds—and to make the most inane conversation that is humanly possible. At recreation, too, order
of precedence was observed, and I, being not even a
postulant, was the lowest of all, and would have walked
behind the lay sisters had they not insisted that I walk
beside them. And the lay sisters enchanted me more
than any of the other nuns, especially Soeur Marie
Emilie. Of her I wrote in *The Flowering Tree*:

Soeur Marie Emilie
is little and very old:

her eyes are onyx
and her cheeks vermilion,
her apron wide and kind
and cobalt blue.

She comforts
generations and generations
of children
who are "new"
at the convent school.
When they are eight
they are already up to her shoulder:
they grow up and go into the world;
she remains
for ever,
already incredibly old,
but, incredibly, never older.

Generations of children
sit in turn by her side
and help her to shell the peas;
her dry and twisted fingers crackle,
snapping the green pods;
generations of children
sit in turn by her side,
helping to stone the plums
that will be made into jam,
for the greater glory of God.

She has affinity with the hens.
When a hen dies,
she sits down on a bench and cries;

she is the only grown-up whose tears
are not frightening tears.
Children can weep
without shame
at her side.
She is simple as flax.
She collects the eggs;
they are warm and smooth
and softly coloured,
ivory, ochre,
and brown and rose.

We have grown up
and gone away
"into the world"
and grown cold
in the service of God,
but we would love Him
even less than we do
if we had never known
Soeur Marie Emilie,
with the green peas and the plums,
and the hens and the beautiful eggs,
and her apron as wide and kind
as skies on a summer day,
and as clean and blue.

It was joy unspeakable to go with Soeur Marie Emilie
to collect the eggs and to see them, warm, rosy, gold and
white in her hard brown hand, or to listen to her positively lyrical conversations with the hens and the dog—

joy, too, to go as I did nearly every day to help the lay sisters and some of the younger nuns to "prepare the little jams," which meant stoning the plums for jam-making. This was done in silence; we each had a saucer of plums, and a big tin was put into the middle of the circle to throw the stones into. The only sound was the rattling of the stones as we threw them in.

It was considered a "sin against poverty" to break a saucer. Whether there was some nervous tension about this which I felt, I don't know, but I became possessed by an unholy desire to break one on purpose. This became a kind of compulsive obsession, until one day I did it. I took my saucer and threw it down on the stone yard where we were working, breaking it to pieces. Everyone stared at me, aghast; no one spoke. One lay sister leaned over to me and patted my hand kindly. Then I got up and walked stiffly to the Reverend Mother's room to confess what I had done and that I had done it deliberately.

She nodded silently several times and then said gently, "I sink you must have some more of fun—you are a child."

For several days, instead of preparing the little jams, I walked in the vegetable garden with the Reverend Mother, who exhorted me to "regard the little cabbages, how in their way they praise God."

It was during the summer holidays that the 1914-18 war broke out.

Many of the old nuns remembered the Franco-Prussian war of 1870, and had frequently told us of their terrible ordeals during the German occupation, especially in Alsace and Lorraine. One grand old lady in particular never tired of repeating stories of how, as a child, she lived underground hidden in a sewer and fed on rats and mice. No sooner was war declared than the nuns, anticipating immediate famine, put themselves on iron rations. My sister and I were put on something approaching iron rations too.

As soon as the school reassembled, by which time the war must have been getting well under way, we gathered in the hall to sing the *Marseillaise,* led by our headmistress, a large nun who, both in her face and her rather amazing gait, loose-limbed and almost double-jointed, resembled a pantomime horse; stamping to and fro before the assembled school, she worked herself and us into a frenzy worthy of the Bastille. This was repeated daily. Everywhere in the school, maps were pinned up, showing the battlefields and studded with little flags, to indicate the positions of the German and French armies, before which we shuddered or exulted, according to whether we had to increase the number of German or French flags. Patriotism and religion became inextricably mixed, the war a Crusade, a holy war; every French soldier who died on the battlefield, a martyr.

The children flung aside their silk embroideries and began to knit furiously—woollen helmets, woollen socks, woollen mittens for soldiers; only I failed to knit anything that would not have *added* to the hardship of trench warfare, and so turned my attention to composing patriotic poetry and hymns. One of my hymns was set to music by a nun and sung in the chapel, which made my head swell to the size of a Zeppelin.

We were indoctrinated with fierce hatred of the Germans, hatred accelerated by the bitter memories that still haunted the older nuns and sharpened their dread of a German invasion of England; hatred which blazed up more and more relentlessly as, day after day, appalling lists of casualties were published, and news came of the death on the sacred soil of the French battlefields of the brothers and fathers and nephews of the nuns and the French schoolgirls; hatred which, I fear, despite our own avowed wish to be martyrs in the cause of the *entente cordiale,* was encouraged by the almost uneatable food that was now put on the table and attributed to the wickedness of the Germans. Soon little Belgian refugees poured into England, and several came to the convent. They too had lurid stories to tell which added fuel to the fires of our hatred.

It was at this time that I had an experience, lasting for probably less than half a minute and almost indescribable, but one which was to influence the rest of my life.

I have told you that with two exceptions the community consisted of French and Belgian women. The exceptions were the young English nun and one lay sister who was Bavarian. To us, Bavarian meant German. She had always, I think, been rather a lonely woman.

She spoke hardly any English at all, and deplorable French. She had no such affinity with animals as Soeur Marie Emilie had, no charm or talent like another of the lay sisters who was a beautiful woman with a beautiful singing voice; and she had, of course, no friends or relations with whom she could make any contact now, and no letters. Even among the children she had no real contacts. She understood what they said, but they could not understand what she said, either in German or French, and she had so little English—and, unhappily, no charm. What her loneliness must have been when the war had broken out, I cannot imagine.

One day I was passing the boot-room, the little room where our shoes were kept; the door was open, and the Bavarian nun was sitting alone, cleaning shoes. I can see her now as if it were yesterday—a tall, gaunt woman with brilliantly red cheeks and eyes so dark that they looked black: there she was, wearing her large, cobalt-blue apron, with a child's pair of shoes on her lap.

I stopped and went in, intending to help her to polish the shoes. It was only when I had come quite close to her that I saw that she was weeping; tears were running down her rosy cheeks and falling onto the blue apron and the child's shoes. Abashed, I dropped my eyes and stood in front of her, speechless with embarrassment, completely tongue-tied. I saw her large, toilworn hands come down onto her lap and fold on the little shoes, and even those hands, red and chapped, with blunted nails, were folded in a way that expressed inconsolable grief.

We were both quite silent, I staring down at her beautiful hands, afraid to look up, not knowing what to say; she weeping soundlessly.

At last, with an effort, I raised my head, and then—I saw—the nun was crowned with the crown of thorns.

I shall not attempt to explain this. I am simply telling the thing as I saw it.

That bowed head was weighed under the crown of thorns.

I stood for—I suppose—a few seconds, dumbfounded, and then, finding my tongue, I said to her, "*I* would not cry, if I was wearing the crown of thorns like you are."

She looked at me as if she were startled, and asked, "What you mean?"

"I don't know," I said, and at the time I did not.

I sat down beside her, and together we polished the shoes.

Chapter 7

When I was between fourteen and fifteen years old I left my French convent in floods of tears to go to my mother in London.

Since the end of my first term I had become increasingly ill, with mysterious pains that the school doctor could not or would not diagnose. He was an old man with a vast beard which was dyed ginger and on rainy days dripped ginger spots onto our bodies when he examined us. He held firmly to the belief that children were incorrigible malingerers, shamming to avoid lessons. I, having already been suspected of neurosis before I came to school, stood no chance with him at all. When I began to starve myself, it became certain that I was either naughty or neurotic—which in those days was generally considered to be the same thing. The poor man ordered me to go to my lessons, play games and eat my food.

The Reverend Mother, however, refused to send me to classes, though there was nothing I longed for more myself than to learn. I refused to play games and was never made to do so, and for a long time I succeeded in passing nearly all of my food under the table to other children. As I did not get thin, but on the contrary fat, it was not for a very long time that I was discovered, and by that time I really could not digest ordinary food.

The Reverend Mother would not accept the idea that I was shamming, and could not, because of the doctor's verdict, insist that I was not, so she treated me as an invalid, and incidentally rather as if I were "Little Nellie of Holy God," the saintly and precocious little Irish girl who, when she was about four years old, edified the entire community of the convent orphanage in which she lived, and who was continually held up to us as an example. I walked in the garden for most of my time until, owing to the mysterious pains, I could not walk at all. Then I was befriended by a grand old nun who taught painting. She was an aristocrat, a mystic, and a fine artist, incredibly severe, because, I think, of the true artist's inability to be satisfied by anything but perfection. She had the appearance of a fierce owl about to pounce on its prey.

To her "art room" I went daily and became absorbed

in endless drawings of Hiawatha. These delighted another nun into whose special care I was given, the meekest person I have ever known, with an incurable habit of blushing when she was looked at. We children, with the cruelty children usually show to anyone defenceless, used to stare at her until she was literally crimson and her eyes filled with tears. She delighted in Hiawatha because she secretly longed to be a Red Indian! When I was moved from the big dormitory to a little one that she presided over, and in which there was usually no other child but myself, she used to tell me astonishingly bloodthirsty stories about Red Indians, invented by herself.

The "pale-faced nun" of my rhythm had also become an invalid, and I was allowed to go and see her, in a little room she now occupied alone, every day. I was deeply attached to her, and it was indeed she who taught me "the lesson of sacrifice," by her own magnificent attitude to suffering and visible love of God—I think, too, by her tenderness to me.

In consequence of these things, when I left to go to London, I had learnt no more, except about religion and painting, than Smoky had taught me before I went to school.

In London, after I had been taken to several doctors who disagreed, my uncle (the one who baptised me in the salad bowl) decided to settle the matter once and for all by performing an exploratory operation. He did so, and I was acquitted of the charge of shamming. A long-standing diseased appendix with resultant internal complications was discovered.

I will speak briefly of the next two schools I was sent to, and I speak of them at all only because they gave me a distaste for the Protestant religion, not because I found anything wrong in it at the time or ever thought about it, but because it produced (or so I thought) an atmosphere of deadly boredom—just as the nuns' poverty and love of God had produced an atmosphere of almost sacramental loveliness. The two Protestant schools both had the effect of saturating me with boredom, though they were totally different from each other.

The first, to which I was sent as a day scholar, was a very big kind of Council school in the heart of London. I have never been in an uglier place. It was as bare as the convent but had none of the shining polish and spotless white curtains, none of the convent smell of beeswax and linen and flowers—just bare, rough and dirty unpolished boards, benches and tables, and a yard for a playground, surrounded by high brick walls like a prison yard. To complete the feeling of being in prison, we were addressed by numbers, not by our names.

There were about fifty pupils in each class, and none of them received any individual attention. I, having had no general education at all, and being put into my class simply because it was the grade that I ought to have made at the age of fourteen, understood not one word of the lessons.

This school reawakened my attitude of defiance to authority, and I behaved outrageously. When addressed by my number I refused to answer, and the teacher's rage failed to make me speak a word, or to stand up. At lunch, which we took in the school, I refused to eat anything at all. In the yard I refused to play with, or to speak to, any of the children except the Jewish ones.

The Catholics and the Jews were always sent out of the room during the daily school prayers, and this pleased me. The Pharisee in me was rearing its head, and already I was saying to myself in this school, "Thank God I am not as other men!" I considered the Jews vastly superior to the Protestants, and being the only Catholic myself, as my sister did not attend the school, I was glad to be numbered with them.

I remained only for a week. Evidently after a day or two the teachers, who probably thought that I was half-witted, decided not to bother about me and simply ignored me. I was furious that my defiance no longer seemed to disturb them, so I decided to leave altogether. My mother insisted on my starting for school in the morning, so I spent the days reading books on the counters of book-shops until the headmistress wrote for an explanation of my absence. Then my mother allowed me to leave the school.

I was still in poor health, so it was decided that I was to be sent as a boarder to a tiny private Protestant school at the seaside; but once more, on the doctor's orders this time, I was forbidden to attend classes.

This little school was kept by a sweet elderly lady of some intelligence, and her silly but amiable sister. I think that they both knew less about real life outside their select school than the older—and even some of the younger—of their pupils.

I had absolutely nothing to do here and was acutely bored. The headmistress, who had undertaken to see that I practised my religion, was most conscientious about this and delegated a young French teacher to take me to church every day; the French teacher herself had said that it should be every day because she was really a *non-pratiquante* Catholic who only professed her faith at all in order to get out of the Protestant services and devotions which played a large part in the school life. She had a further motive, namely friends in the town to whom she found it diverting to pay a daily visit. Horror-stricken at being a party to this deceit, I tried to salve my conscience by making the daily visit to the church myself, and the Blessed Sacrament was the greatest link with my old convent, for which I was still homesick.

Boredom became almost a disease with me, and I wrote to my mother, asking her to let me come home. She refused, so I wrote to Smoky, asking him to send me the railway fare; then, leaving a polite letter to the headmistress thanking her for her kindness and apologising for my ingratitude, I went home.

By this time—and I think the intelligent reader need not be told this!—I had indeed become "singular." I was a prig and a pious prig, and, in my way, an intellectual snob. With Smoky, who still brought the poets and philosophers to life for me and who still showed me the poetry and beauty of my faith, I was happy, but with no one else. I realised that I must seem odd to other children and became acutely self-conscious about it.

My mother, no doubt distracted because of my behaviour and worried because I was openly pining for the French convent, forbade me to have any correspondence with anyone there at all, and I became more and more introverted and lonely. I refused to go out of the house whenever I possibly could, and spent my whole time writing poetry, a habit which exasperated my mother. I did not then wish for any friendship with other girls of my age, and dreaded all their games and interests, which I thought would interfere with my writing. I had in fact become a maladjusted child, and, knowing it, tried by every means in my power to avoid the company of other people.

Then I became ill again, really ill, though how far the illness was induced by psychological factors I don't know. It was largely digestive, and I again refused to eat. I had to have treatment which embarrassed me and which meant going into a nursing home.

This time I was sent to a little home in Brighton, in order that I could be put into the care of Dr. Paley once again, the doctor who had played so big a part in my becoming a Catholic and who had known me from my early childhood. I think there were only four or five patients there, all of them chronically but none of them critically ill. The old retired nurse who kept the home was a Presbyterian. She was a very kind woman and very patient with me, but used to bore and exasperate me by continual preaching about "counting your blessings" and a daily spate of similar platitudes. I was kept in bed for several months, during which period she sat in my room for an hour or so daily and depressed me beyond words by her righteousness.

There was only one other nurse in the home, a large, over-cheerful young woman with teeth like a horse's, feet at right angles, and no conversation at all. She was very good-natured and very long-suffering; it was she who carried out the, to me, appalling and embarrassing treatment to which I was submitted, and later, when I was recovering, pushed me out in a bath chair, to drink cups of chocolate and eat cakes in cafés. When it came to the question of food she found her tongue and became quite eloquent.

No Catholic priest ever visited me in the home (probably none knew that a Catholic was there), but an old Protestant clergyman, who visited the other patients regularly, always came to see me too. He was a very kind man and had a deep love for Our Lord, which he was able to impart to me in some measure. His life had been darkened by tragedy; his daughter and only child had been taken away by white slave traffickers. I did not realise what this meant, excepting that she had been kidnapped, but I did realise the suffering of the kind old man, and I was always deeply impressed by people who could suffer bitterly without becoming bitter themselves. He was such a one.

At first Dr. Paley allowed me to be alone, but when the physical side of my illness was more or less cured he sent his daughter, who was grown up but young, to see me, and she with infinite tact introduced me once more into their household, where I had spent so much of my babyhood. There, in the Paleys' house, I found again the beauty that meant so much to me, and was among people who loved the things that I loved— poetry, art, books. They loved music too, but I did not. I was surrounded too by understanding and affection; here I was made to feel welcome and not to feel myself a freak. I was shy but not tortured by shyness. Nevertheless I was still unable to face and accept the normal life of an adolescent, and Dr. Paley, with great wisdom and kindness that I did not yet appreciate, dropped what was a bombshell for me. He said that the time had now come when I must either adjust myself to life or become a chronic invalid. The only thing to do was to send me to a boarding school again, but this time to a big convent school with a hundred boarders. It was a case of kill or cure, and, Dr. Paley said, my only chance.

Chapter 8

When I went to my English convent I was fifteen years old. I had lived for nearly a year an almost solitary life, and at that the life of an invalid. I was a confirmed prig and morbidly shy. Even in my own home I could not bring myself to enter a room in which there were other people, even people I knew well. until I had first gone to the door two or three times and failed to force myself to walk in. I definitely had become that which is above all things suspect in the type of convent I had now come to—"singular": and I was more "singular" in this environment than I would have been in any other.

I had more than my fair share of the intolerance of youth, which—conflicting with painful awareness of my own shortcomings and my inability, and indeed my unwillingness, to adjust myself to normal people of my own age—produced a bravado in me that must have seemed to be intolerable conceit. My old tendency to revolt against authority was reawakened by the formalism characteristic of this community, and by the many conventions and traditions of the school. Unable to feel myself one with the society into which I was now thrown against my will, I became anti-social and in revolt against *everything* that restrained my own oddities. This was, of course, a defence mechanism of a humiliated person, one who was humiliated by being herself and therefore really defenceless.

Looking back, I am astonished by the kindness with which I was treated by my schoolfellows, by every one of them without an exception.

I was not sent to this school to finish my education; indeed, my general education had not really begun; I was sent for the sake of the seaside air for my health, and as a "kill or cure" method of forcing me to adjust myself to other people.

I was to be there as an exception to nearly everything: I was only to attend classes when I wanted to, I was only to study if and when I felt inclined, I was not to play games—this exception alone would have been sufficient to make me unpopular; but I added to it by assuming an air of superiority, doubtless to cover my real inferiority, and by saying and doing everything I possibly could to provoke the dislike of my schoolfellows. There were a hundred of them, and though my background must have been as unknown to them as theirs was to me, and I was the very incarnation of everything that embarrasses English adolescents and even disgusts them, I do not remember one single occasion when one of those hundred girls ever said or did anything to me that was not tolerant and kind. On the contrary, during the year I spent there everyone went out of her way to help and befriend me.

Everything in this convent was in complete contrast to my French convent. That was small, this was big. The nuns there had been almost a motley community in their informality, here they were extremely formal, and a great deal of formality was imposed upon the children. Both nuns and girls, it seemed, must have a particular character, even a particular manner, stamped on them. We were drilled over and over again, during the first week of term, for our coming in and out of chapel, until we were all able to make every genuflection, and almost every movement, in exactly the same way, and at exactly the same time, with the precision and impersonality of machinery.

Open piety was considered to be in bad taste; the spontaneous, possibly rather raggle-taggle, visits to the Blessed Sacrament encouraged in the French convent were not encouraged or even allowed here. We could not without special permission visit the chapel excepting "in ranks" for official services and visits, and it would have been thought "singular" to ask for the permission more than very occasionally. I fancy that Children of Mary had some special privileges in this respect, but as I always had a "bad spirit" instead of "the spirit of the school," I was excluded from that sodality. Even our handwriting had to be as far as possible uniform, and characteristic not of ourselves but of the Order. We were given specimens of several nuns' writing and made to copy them, like small children learning script in a kindergarten.

In the French convent, you will remember, it was forbidden to speak of your family; here, on the contrary, family was a constant topic of conversation, and it was talked of in a way suggesting that most of the children were possessed both of grandeur and wealth.

For example, horses were talked about so much that my first, though short, impression was that they were the *only* subject that interested my schoolfellows. The general horsiness was shared by many of the nuns, and stories were continually circulated about how magnificently Mother So-and-So had ridden to hounds "in the world," or how Mother So-and-So, on the night before she entered, had kissed, not her mother, but the warm, soft nose of her favourite hunter.

Most of the nuns, and most of the pupils too, seemed to be drawn from a number of "good Catholic families" —"good" in the social sense. These families were constantly spoken about, not only in connection with the girls but the nuns too, for naturally nearly everyone had an aunt or some other relative in the community. In some cases when a nun was of very aristocratic family her family name was used, added on to her name in religion.

I observed, too, that if a dead nun had belonged to a "good" or celebrated family, she would be an almost certain candidate for a biography, on the grounds that she had been outstandingly holy. All this network of family had an inevitable bearing on the traditions of the school, and I do not think it unfair to say that, though few of them would ever have questioned their faith, they held it unconsciously, and were proud of it more as family tradition than as a personal conviction. This sometimes resulted in narrowness and exclusiveness.

It is possible that some people would think that the stress put on the value of suffering in the French convent tended to be overdone, especially as joy, which was of course valued there too, was usually represented as purely spiritual joy. Possibly in my case, as I was ill, I heard more about the meaning of suffering than I would have done otherwise. Be that as it may, in this convent, that which I had formerly been taught to think of as the "pride of life," but which was really just the exuberance of good health, was considered much more desirable than suffering. The standard of health was in fact wonderful, which was the main reason why this school was chosen for me, but I was bewildered by the sportiness and heartiness, the healthiness and wealthiness and horsiness, of nearly all my schoolfellows.

88

In my French convent I had been taught to reverence poverty and humility almost more than any other virtue, and certainly poverty had radiated a lyrical beauty of its own. In my new convent it seemed to me that everything and everyone was rich, and that it was thought a virtue to be rich. I suppose there must have been some poor people there, but at the time I thought myself to be the only one. The others always seemed to have money to spend lavishly in the school shop and to meet the continual demands that were made on us. I came with only a few shillings, tips given to me by my father and Smoky. After the first week I had nothing left.

At that time my mother was working for her living in London, and even had I not been brought up to think it unpardonable to ask my parents or anyone else —except, in a real emergency, Smoky—for money, I would then have been too sensitive to ask. I remained embarrassed by my lack of it, which increased my self-consciousness until the end of my school life, and beyond it. It was not simply the fact that everyone but myself seemed to *have* money that puzzled me, but that no one seemed to *understand* money. Both nuns and pupils gave me the impression that they believed that it fell like manna from Heaven. They seemed unable to realise that there really were people in this world, other than those who at that time lined up at soup kitchens and received "charity," who literally had *no* money at all, excepting what they could earn. It seemed, too, to be taken for granted that when we left school we would all be rich. We were not taught, or even allowed, to mend our own clothes or darn our own stockings, it being supposed that we would always have maids to do it for us.

I think that this blind spot about money is common to very many nuns, and that today, even more than when I was young, it is, though an understandable thing, a very serious one. I shall return to it later in another connection.

Yet another contrast between the old school and the new one was the attitude to games. Here, though art, music and the theatricals were considered to be important, especially theatricals, games were, on the whole, thought to be more so, especially by the children.

I had an almost fanatical, certainly a neurotic, dislike for sport which dated from long before I went to school at all, and I think began in the days of my earliest memories when I was taken to watch my mother, a champion at every game, in turn playing hockey, then tennis, and then golf. A very early memory is seeing a remarkably bloody incident on the hockey field, in which a woman lost her eye. To me, sport seemed to be simply an outlet for savagery and brutality. Doubtless my own physical inability to take part in it, and the knowledge that this constituted human failure in my mother's eyes, added to my determination to condemn it as morally wrong. I not only refused to play, but even to pray about the school matches, even to watch them, and I sneered openly at the general enthusiasm. Even this did not provoke my schoolfellows to give me the snubbing that I deserved.

Arrogant though I was, I did not presume to judge, let alone condemn, my schoolfellows or the nuns, but I was bewildered, really baffled, by the contrast between this convent and the last one. I had been taught that one of the main proofs of the divine origin of the Church is that "she is one." I had a complete misconception of what this meant, and thought that it must necessarily mean that at least all religious Orders were exactly like each other in essential things, that poverty, humility, unworldliness would express themselves outwardly, as well as inwardly, in the same way everywhere and in every Order. It was a far cry then, to the day in which I was to learn how infinitely inclusive "the Body of Christ on earth" really is. As I saw it with my limited experience and knowledge, my two convents might have represented two different religions, not, as they really did, two different temperaments, the French and the English, among a countless number of temperaments which are all one in the inclusiveness of Christ.

Had I imagined myself to be surrounded by sinners, I would have been less bewildered, because I remembered Smoky's argument to my mother long ago, that only a divinely founded Church could have kept absolute purity of doctrine in spite of the abuses and corruptions that had assailed it through history.

History—that was the word that tripped me up. History, which I knew only through Shakespeare's historical plays, meant for me the Middle Ages. A real sinner, a sinner on the grand scale, who was a true witness to the divine origin of the Church, must be one of those lurid and magnificent sinners of the "Middle Ages"—a Lady Macbeth or a Cesare Borgia.

Although I had suffered, as I have said, from positively neurotic feelings of guilt, I did not presume to rank myself among the great sinners: I had realised that my feelings of guilt were produced by what I felt myself to be (something horrid like a maggot on a cheese), not by something I had done. Real sinners on the grand scale had to be colourful and executive, like the Borgias —or, if they were cloistered sinners, they must be people who buried the skeletons of infants around the place. (As, at fifteen, I did not know the things that are so oddly called "the facts of life," I did not realise the significance of these little skeletons, but I knew that there was something sinister and eerie about them, connected with sin.) Had Our Reverend Mother, in the best Borgia tradition, offered her enemies or her rivals poison, burning crimson in a chalice of gold, or even rattled a little skeleton on the end of her rosary, it would have confirmed my faith. The mediocrity of inculpable snobbery was not enough; it merely bewildered me.

There was one thing which both of my convents had in common—a strict supervision of what we read. In both there was a reasonably good library, but not one including the books I cherished; those which I had brought to school with me were taken away and locked up in a cupboard as being "unsuitable." Among them were Shelley's poems. At that time I had a passion for Shelley similar to the passion for film stars fairly common among schoolgirls today. I knew nothing of his love affairs, smeared as they were by his egoism, or of his hypochondria. To me he was pure flame burning brightly in the cause of beauty and the freedom of the human spirit. Deprived of his poetry, I set about indoctrinating my schoolfellows in Shelley mania.

I was at pains to explain to them that it was not only not wrong of Shelley to have written his pamphlet on the necessity of atheism but that he had been bound in conscience to do so. Just as Smoky, whom I thought to be the most good person in the world, was bound to remain outside the Church because he could not accept the Faith. I went round the school pinning down any girl whom I could persuade to listen to me, and telling her that everyone must be prepared to die if necessary for what he believed to be the truth, even if it was not really the truth at all.

Of course I bored everyone who had the patience to listen to me, and when they told me they were bored and preferred to believe what they were taught rather than to worry about what Shelley did or did not believe, I decided in my arrogance that they were fools, unwilling and perhaps unable to think at all.

I think that I rather wanted to identify myself with Shelley and to imagine myself in the same position that he was in at Eton—not merely, as I really was, a maladjusted adolescent, judging everything from a background of egoism and inexperience, and treated with toleration and patience that I did not deserve, but as a solitary rebel, standing alone against tyranny, a martyr to the cause of human freedom. I suppose, too, that I was trying to compensate for my ignorance by making an impression about the few things I had learnt. I had not learnt the multiplication tables, the simplest rules of arithmetic, algebra or geometry, anything at all about science, botany or geography. I could not hold my own in any class of children of my own age; hence this desperate attempt to overcompensate on Shelley. It was a deadly failure; nobody was impressed, nobody was interested.

I retired into a kind of sulk and wrote my heart out to Smoky. My letter must have been a masterpiece of uncharitableness. Remembering that Smoky prided himself on not suffering fools gladly, as St. Paul advised the early Christians to do, I declared that neither would I, and that I was hemmed in by them on every side. Having enlarged on that theme, I went on to criticise the nuns, especially the Prefect herself, who represented authority to me. "Mother So-and-So," I said, "thinks that she is the cock of the walk here." (As a matter of fact, she could have been far more truly described as a hen, the hen in the Gospel who loves to gather her chickens under her wings, for she was one of the most loving and motherly women I have ever known, sensitive and tenderhearted almost to a fault, but she hid this, as a rule, under a mask of severity and had the reputation of being a stern disciplinarian.)

A few hours after I had handed my letter to Smoky to her for posting, she sent for me and handed it back. She did not appear to be angry. Had she done so I have no doubt that my rebellious spirit would have hardened, perhaps irrevocably.

There are moments in life, the most critical moments, when one's whole self is in the state of a statue that has been cast in clay and is about to set in a permanent material. Just before the hardening or setting takes place, a single flick of the finger can alter the whole expression for ever, but let that moment pass by so much as a second and the mould is fixed beyond change. Nothing can be done then, if change is desirable, but break it to pieces and begin again. It was one of those moments that this nun gave me—just that flick of the finger which prevented my life from setting in the ugly shape of my adolescence.

Handing my letter back to me, she said, quite gently, "I won't let this go because I cannot allow you to say such unkind things about the children that I love. I love them and Our Lord loves them."

This instantly shamed me; I had not once stopped to think that Our Lord loved these people whom I treated so contemptuously. It was as if my eyes had been opened, and my attitude changed in a flash.

Then the Prefect turned to the part of my letter relating to herself; I was now crimson with shame, but again she was unruffled—indeed, she was smiling.

"About myself," she said, "you are right. I *am* the cock of the walk here, so there is nothing to be done about that but to make the best of it."

Then she told me to go and rewrite the letter, stating the same grievances if I liked, but more justly and more kindly.

It was when I returned to her with the rewritten letter that she made a gesture which I think now was a stroke of genius and did more than almost anything else in my school life to save my faith. She took the new letter and sealed it without reading it. Then she said that, having read the letters between Smoky and myself for several weeks, she had come to the conclusion that I *needed* the outlet of an uncensored correspondence with him, and that he was a perfect friend for me; therefore in future I could hand in my letters to him sealed and would receive his unopened.

It is impossible to overrate the value of that correspondence with Smoky. I had an analytical, hypercritical but very enquiring type of mind, which had been encouraged to be so by Smoky himself from my early childhood; consequently I continued to be perplexed by inconsistencies that I observed, and to demand more and more proofs for the divine origin of the Church. There was a dangerous tendency in my mind to separate the idea of Our Lord and the Blessed Sacrament from the idea of the Church. I had not yet realised the truth

96

of Joan of Arc's "Our Lord and His Church are one," and I knew very little about the Mystical Body of Christ. I was more and more inclined to think of the Church as the hierarchy, bishops and priests, and as a rather rigid authority; I certainly did not know that, in Christ, I myself was as much a part of the Church as the Pope.

My love of Our Lord was strengthened by the Prefect, who talked about Him to me very often privately and allowed me to make many visits to the chapel alone. She had deep understanding even of my faults and "singularity." But I was less fortunate in the school chaplain and in the nun who taught Doctrine.

If religion was something for the heart only, a matter merely of personal feeling and devotion, I would have had nothing to complain of, but for me it had always been of absolute necessity to have an instructed *mind*: without that, religion could not be a thing of the will, which it must be if it is to endure. The school chaplain was a kind but silly old man, with an obsession against sun-bathing, which I suppose was considered shocking in those days. When I told him, as now and then I did in the confessional, that I had "doubts" about the Church, he refused to listen. "Brush them aside like flies" was his invariable answer.

I've no doubt that I was a thorn in the flesh of the nun who taught us Doctrine. I spent a good many hours of my day reading the Gospels and the catechism, and came to the Doctrine class every morning bristling with questions. About this I was perfectly sincere; I really longed for knowledge and put my questions with perfect sincerity. Unhappily the teacher of Doctrine did not believe in my sincerity, and it is not impossible that she found it tiresome, if not difficult, to answer my questions; besides, they held the class up. Most of the scholars were perfectly happy to accept whatever they were taught and to learn the catechism over and over again by heart, and they all had to be ready to give answers, mainly learnt parrot-wise, to an Ecclesiastical Examiner in due course. My volley of questions was a hindrance and nuisance and (the teacher thought) was inspired by insolence.

She snubbed me in class and, taking me aside outside the class, told me that I was impertinent, and that the questions I asked were likely to disturb the faith of the other pupils. This was really providential for me because it led to my writing *all* my questions, doubts and difficulties to Smoky. I might have forgotten the nun's answers to my questions, had she given any, and they might not have impressed me, but I have never forgotten Smoky's, and they exerted a profound influence over me, which is as strong today as it was then.

Perhaps the greatest value of Smoky's letters was that for me they were the beginning of self-knowledge, or at least of a determination to be honest with myself and to know myself as truly as I could. He never gave me a dogmatic answer to anything, but always helped me to think for myself and to find the answers myself. He told me that I was one who wanted the jam without the bread, who wanted the poetry and beauty and peace of religion, but not the discipline; and in that he was right. He wrote as if I were an equal, with none of the patronage that old people often impose upon children, and his letters were not only serious but witty.

With the kindness of my schoolfellows, the wisdom and the genius for love of the Prefect, and with Smoky's letters, I gradually became happy in this convent, in spite of the fact that there was a great deal that was antipathetic to me. Also I regained my health and my appetite. However, no sooner had I become really settled and begun to adjust myself more normally to the other girls than, quite without any warning, I received a letter from my mother telling me that at the end of the term, in about a week's time, I was to come home, and leave school altogether.

Chapter 9

All the way home in the train I tried to guess what reason my mother could have for ordering me to leave school for good at a moment's notice. I was only sixteen and my education, far from having ended, had never really begun. This was 1917, and the war was still going on; there were Zeppelin raids on London day and night, and this, among other reasons, was why I had been sent away.

My curiosity was soon satisfied.

The priest who had given me Holy Viaticum as a child had left his Order and become a secular priest. He was a very sick man both in mind and body, and, not having yet been appointed to a parish, had taken refuge with my mother, in whose home he was now living. My sister was sometimes at home, but more often away at college. My mother still went out to work. I was to come home to act as a chaperone and to help with the housework. This arrangement was intended to be a temporary one, but in fact it continued for a number of years.

During those years I became almost wholly isolated from other Catholics, and struggled, though in the end unsuccessfully, to abandon my religion in favour of some other. This came about partly through my own fault and lack of experience, which led me to judge the whole Catholic world by the behaviour of a handful of individuals.

I was puzzled by the situation at home, but not shocked. It did not occur to me that there was anything morally wrong in it, and I am convinced to this day that there was not. There was nothing new or unusual about my mother collecting a derelict, and derelict the priest was. Not only did I see nothing wrong in the situation, but I did not realise it was unconventional. My mother had always flouted conventions, and I, having spent nearly the whole of my life in convents and nursing homes, had no idea which of them were accepted by people "in the world," or of the savage cruelty which is so readily aroused in certain people when their own cherished conventions are outraged. I was soon to learn. Life with this poor derelict priest was unhappy and very ugly, but what most shocked and puzzled me was not how he treated me, but how his co-religionists treated him: as a matter of fact, their treatment of him was very largely responsible for his treatment of me.

He was an outcast. Only once in the years that followed did one of the many Catholics he had received into the Church visit him with compassion. That visit has stood out in my mind ever since. Very seldom did any priest visit him at all, even when he was desperately ill. Only once, I think, did a member of his late Order come to see him. Those priests who did come, at very rare intervals and for very short visits, showed him no sympathy. Day after day he was pelted by anonymous, and sometimes threatening, letters from (presumably) members of the flock who felt that he had betrayed them. He became more and more of a recluse. Acutely sensitive about his position, which incidentally had been partly brought about by the malicious gossip of righteous people, he refused to come into our social life. He wanted to hide himself.

He forbade me to bring any friends home, and if, as it happened sometimes, one came uninvited, I knew that I would suffer for it. He forbade me, too, to speak of him to anyone outside, or even to another priest in the confessional, telling me that if I did so, he would know it through a curious gift of telepathy. This I believed. He forbade me to write to any Catholic (and I suppose this included non-Catholics) telling them anything about him.

I was not altogether friendless; I still had Smoky,

whom I visited every Saturday and who was wholly charitable to the poor priest, and I still had the friendship of Dr. Paley's family, who gave me the joy of holidays in their home whenever I could go to them; but soon I realised that, apart from having been forbidden to do so, I must not invite any Catholics to come to *my* home, because of *their* attitude.

The tongue of scandal had worked hard and effectively. I had made very few friends at my English convent; those I had made were, with one exception, Argentinians, and had gone back to their own country. The one exception lived at Brighton, and I wrote to her suggesting that when I came there, we should meet. She replied No, she had heard that there was scandal connected with a priest in my home, and therefore neither she nor any member of her family wished to see me again. I felt then that I could not ask any Catholics to meet me even outside my home, without embarrassing *them*, and I ceased to ask them. I felt, too, that in spite of the genuine love bestowed on me by the Paley family, and the beauty and joy that this brought into my life, I must really be wronging them by staying in their house. I would at this time have severed this connection, as I did all my other Catholic relationships, but for Smoky, who persuaded me that as their love was genuine and long proven, I would hurt them deeply by refusing their invitations. He warned me that I must not judge Catholics as a whole by the conduct of "a few Pharisees." He reminded me, too, of his argument about the abuses within the Church proving its divine origin, but this failed to help me now, for the same reason that it had done in my English convent—namely, that although I was bewildered by the attitude of these bigoted Catholics, I did not think of them as "sinners." On the contrary, their very "churchiness" led me to think that they were what they evidently supposed themselves to be—the cream of Catholicism. That *they* condemned our poor derelict as a sinner was obvious, though I do not, and did not, think he was that myself.

It was precisely this that shocked me—that people who *were* "good Catholics," who, as some of these did, took the lead in all the parish activities and were known to be descended from "good Catholic families," should be hard, censorious and indeed cruel and vindictive towards one whom they regarded as a sinner, and who was in fact an outcast. To put this plainly, I was appalled by the fact, as it then in my teens appeared to me, that people could be "good Catholics" and yet not *Christians*. I had yet to learn the extreme of God's love which makes it possible that even one whose life is not Christian in practice can be more than Christian, he can be "a Christ," though it may be a Christ crucified, or entombed in a human life.

To young and inexperienced people a single word or gesture can produce an emotional reaction which has unimaginable consequences; certainly, before one is twenty these often thoughtless incidents are more effective than any reasoning. Such a one precipitated a crisis for me. One morning, quite by chance, I knelt at Holy Communion side by side with two people, a husband and wife, who had in the past been acquainted with my mother and the priest she now harboured. They were highly respected Catholics. After Mass I greeted them in the church porch. They ignored my greeting and turned away.

From that moment I made up my mind to seek for some other religion. I did not doubt the Real Presence in the Blessed Sacrament, but it seemed to me that Christ was a prisoner in the hands of hard and relentless people, people without compassion. I began to hope that there might be some other Church in which there would also be the Real Presence, but in which one could approach and receive Christ, not among respectable people, not among censorious people, but among those who were despised, who were failures, who were sinners, but who loved one another. That "good Catholics" should receive Communion side by side with one whom they immediately cut dead, appalled me. It appalled me that it was into the hands of such that, so it seemed to me, Christ had given Himself—"this night you will all be scandalised in Me."

There was another reason, too, why I had at this time withdrawn myself from those Catholic friends who would most certainly have treated me with sympathy, including the nuns at my English convent (you will remember that I had long ago been forbidden to communicate with the French ones).

This was money. I have mentioned the blind spot

about money that I found in the English convent. I want to make it clear that since those days I have known many nuns who have *not* that blind spot, and that even among those to whom I am referring there were individual nuns who had not, and who in fact helped poor people in ways that were hidden for the very reason that they were tactful and delicate. But the fact remains, the majority of the nuns and girls in that school did not realise, or seemed not to, that there can be people in this world, other than those in a soup kitchen or workhouse, who have no money at all.

But *I* had no money at all, except the occasional presents of ten shillings or so that I received on birthdays. Friendship with any nun who did not know this was beyond my means. I had not, as a rule, even the coppers to pay bus fares—let alone, as nuns often seemed to assume, money for taxis. If the upkeep of friendship with a nun did not equal that of a small car, it did that of a bicycle, and it was out of my reach. I could never be sure of keeping an appointment in time. I often had to walk long distances to keep them at all, and to keep a nun waiting and waste *her* time was thought to be the very height of discourtesy.

As to attending the meetings and reunions of "old girls," this, too, bristled with embarrassments that my vanity shrank from. Large subscriptions were *demanded* of us, usually publicly and tactlessly; I had not the humility to admit my *un*holy poverty. Neither had I any but the oldest and shabbiest clothes, and I burnt with the memory that a nun had once said to me that to go to a house as a guest shabbily and unsuitably dressed embarrassed the hostess and was unpardonable. Consequently I dropped the Catholic friends who might have saved me from what now became a flight from Catholicism, and I dropped them without a word of explanation, in a way that must have seemed callous and ungrateful.

It is a matter of astonishment to me that when I resumed relationship with these nuns years later, no explanation was asked from me, and I was welcomed as kindly as if there had been no interval at all.

I still went to Mass on Sundays. But now I was beginning to ask myself if I should not stop doing so until I had solved what had now become a real conflict in my mind about the Church. The liturgy appealed to me deeply, and as everything in my home was ugly, it was the only real beauty in my life. The Blessed Sacrament still drew me like a magnet. But I began to ask myself —how could I think clearly, how could I judge clearly, so long as I was under the spell of the beauty of the liturgy? Later, when I was an art student, I became, like nearly every other art student I have ever known, obsessed by the Russian Ballet, but at this time the liturgy, the Mass in particular, was the only thing that redeemed the greyness and dullness of my life. While I was wrestling with myself—should I or should I not compel myself to give up going to Mass?—an incident occurred which decided the matter for me.

In those days there were one or two churches in

London which still kept the custom of making specific charges for seats. There were free seats too, but if one arrived too late to fill one, one was charged sixpence or a shilling. I was not allowed to set out for Mass until after I had made the beds and done the washing-up at home. Sometimes, as on this particular day, this meant that I could only go to a church where there was a Mass at twelve o'clock. This in its turn meant a long walk. There was no local Mass at twelve o'clock.

On this day I set out, without a penny in my pocket, to walk to a twelve o'clock Mass in a fashionable district. It was a considerable distance from my home, and I arrived only just in time. Alas, all the free seats were taken. I looked round in confusion and saw that there was just one empty seat among the sixpennies, and slipped into that.

I had scarcely knelt down and hidden my face, which was scarlet, when the verger prodded me in the ribs with a collecting bag on the end of a long cane.

"I will go up to the altar of God," said the priest at the altar. "To God, the giver of youth and happiness."

"Sixpence," said the verger, and prodded me again.

I looked up and shook my head.

"Sixpence," said the verger, and went on prodding.

"I haven't got sixpence," I whispered.

"All right, then," said the verger, "you must go into the free seats."

"There isn't one," I said.

"Well, then, sixpence."

I was scalded. There was a priest standing in the aisle watching the scene. When I sprang to my feet and pushed out of the sixpenny seats, he came forward and put his hand on my shoulder.

"You are not going, child?" he said. I shook him off.

"Yes, I am, and I will never come to Mass again."

I went, beginning the long walk home again, hardly able to stop my tears of rage.

"Thou, O God, art all my strength, why hast thou cast me off?" said the priest at the altar. "Why do I go mourning, with enemies pressing me hard?"

Chapter 10

The murder of the Russian Emperor and his family took place in a cellar in Ekaterinburg on the night of July 17th, 1918.

On that night it was raining in London. Although it was summer, it was a sad grey evening. I was sent out to buy some potatoes at the corner of the street we lived in; a dull, drab street it was, too, a long street of tall grey houses which had once been rich but were now on their way to falling into the dereliction of slums. I should have been back in ten minutes, but something happened which detained me and brought me a considerable scolding. It was, however, the first scolding of my life of which I was almost unaware. Something had filled my consciousness to the exclusion of everything else. Before describing this I must make an explanation.

I have already told you about the Bavarian lay sister in my French convent whom I saw crowned with thorns.

What do I mean by saying that "I saw"? Frankly, in the ordinary way I did not *see* anything at all; at least I did not see anything with my eyes. So far as my eyes were concerned, it was just the same nun, gaunt and rosy, with tears running down her cheeks, but—and this is difficult if not impossible to explain—I saw her *with my mind* wearing the crown of thorns, and saw this vividly in detail, in a way that is unforgettable, though in fact it was something suddenly *known,* rather than seen. But it was known not as one knows something through learning about it, but simply by *seeing* it. Perhaps I could say in the way a child learns something from looking at a picture, but in this case it is not a lifeless picture that can be shut up in a book, but a picture that is alive and fills the world, that is even more vivid, more unforgettable, because it is seen with the mind, not with the eyes.

It was such an experience that I had on that night in July 1918, one which I now know to have been linked with the first of its kind for me, the Bavarian nun crowned with the crown of thorns.

I was on my way to buy potatoes, hurrying because I had been warned that they were wanted for dinner, and so I must not linger. Suddenly I was held still, as if a magnet held my feet to a particular spot in the middle of the road. In front of me, above me, literally wiping out not only the grey street and sky but the whole world, was something which I can only call a gigantic and living Russian icon. I had never seen a Russian icon at the time, nor, I think, any reproduction of one. I have seen very many since, but none that has approached this one in beauty.

It was an icon of Christ the King crucified.

Stretched on a cross of fire in a vestment which blazed and flamed with jewels, crowned with a great crown of gold which weighed His head down, Christ was lifted above the world in our drab street, lifted up and filling the sky. His arms reaching, as it seemed, from one end of the world to the other, the wounds on His hands and feet rubies, but molten rubies that bled with light. Everything, even the glowing folds of the vestments, seemed to be burning and stirring with life and movement as flames of fire do; the spread arms with the long, stretched hands tapering from the jewelled sleeves were like gorgeous wings covering the world; Christ Himself, with His head bowed down by the crown, brooding over the world. In the midst of this splendour the austere simplicity of that beautiful face stood sharp with grief. But the eyes and the mouth smiled with the ineffable love which consumes sorrow and pain as rags are consumed in a burning fire.

I do not know for how long I stood there or how long this impression lasted. I think it could not have been more than a few minutes, as when it was over, though the street was in dusk, it was not quite dark.

I was embarrassed to find, when I reached the vegetable shop, that tears were running down my face. The kind woman who sold me the potatoes tried to comfort me, supposing, I imagine, that I was in some kind of trouble, but I could not stop those tears. Finally she gave me an apple as a present, and I went home.

I do not know how soon after that the news of the assassination of the Tsar was published—it might have been the next day. I only know that when I went out again and saw, at the same street corner where I had seen the crucified king, a placard proclaiming the assassination of the Russian Tsar, I knew the meaning of what I had seen more vividly. For the face of the Tsar in the newspaper photographs was the face of my Christ the King, but without its glory.

From that moment I was completely dominated by the thought of Russia. Russia became for me the country in which the Passion of Christ was being lived out. Because of the seed of martyrs' blood being sown there, and above all because of the anointed king's blood sacrilegiously shed there, I was convinced that Christ, whom I saw as descending upon the world and into the lives of men to be crucified in them, would return to the world to take possession of all mankind through Russia, that the conversion of the world to Christ (I did not at that time say to Catholicism) would begin, indeed *had* begun, in "Holy Russia" with the murder of her king.

This seeing of the "icon of Christ the King" had a profound effect on my attitude to other people.

113

In spite of the early teaching of the French convent that humiliation can be the way to the glory of God, I had failed to accept the humiliations that had been heaped upon me; my heart had contracted, my mind narrowed. As most humiliated and self-centred people do, I resented not only those people who had in fact snubbed me, but those who possessed what I lacked; and like most of those who are vain and secretly scourged by awareness of their own inferiority, my inclination was rather to drag people down to my level, if I could, than to make any effort to lift myself up to theirs.

I delighted in reading the Gospel that what one did to those who were hungry, thirsty, naked and homeless was done to Christ, and found no difficulty in identifying Christ with those who shared my own circumstances. The "Christianity" which I had been searching for was becoming more and more tainted by a socialistic tendency, and if not class-consciousness, at least money-consciousness. Christ Himself in my mind began to belong to one class of people only, those who were poor, and who in my ignorance I supposed were despised by the rich. No doubt at the root of this tendency was the simple fact that among very poor people I was not humiliated myself by my own poverty. I had set my face against the rich, whom I supposed to be the "idle" classes, and was becoming more and more anti-clerical, with a growing dislike for every hierarchy.

Now suddenly, between one heart-beat and the next, I had seen the drama and reality of Christ's Passion in kings. While I stood in my London street on my way to buy potatoes, a king in Russia had died Christ's death. The tragedy and the terrible beauty of it had entered into my soul; it had entered my heart too, like a spear of burning light, and opened it. I became in an instant deeply aware of the sacrilege involved in murdering an anointed king, and the name Christ—"The Anointed" —was suddenly overwhelmingly significant to me.

At the same moment I had a premonition of the things that were to come, of the vast stretch and anguish of the Passion of Christ in which the kings of the world, the hierarchies, and the common people would be one, in one terrible glory.

I was profoundly ignorant. Concerning the personal character of the Tsar of Russia or any of his family I knew nothing. But it had become a reality to me, and that in the flash of a second, that the Tsar was a great deal more than one man, one king. In him in some inexplicable way was kingship itself, and that kingship was made doubly holy by the certainty which took possession of me that he was to be a martyr. It was not that one man alone, but a long line, a kind of dynasty of martyrs that drew my heart. The blood of kings was to fall crimson on Russian snows, but mingled with it the blood of peasants, raised by their martyrdom to kingship; and from that great vivifying stream would flow the blood of martyrs all over the world, redeeming the world.

It was not for nothing that my first glimpse of Christ

in man was in the humblest of lay sisters, bowed by a great crown of thorns, and my second a king in splendour, bowed under a great crown of gold. I realised that every crown is Christ's crown, and the crown of gold is a crown of thorns.

Chapter 11

At the time when I saw the "Russian icon" of Christ the King Crucified over London, and indeed over the world, it was only about a year since I had left my second convent school. But in that time my background had changed completely.

I was—partly through my own fault, as I have said— cut off from nearly all my Catholic friends, and those I had not fled from I saw but seldom. My one really solid friend was still Smoky; he, a man of inexhaustible charity and justice, in spite of his irritability, with its false impression of intolerance, never condemned the poor priest in our house, and indeed always welcomed him to his own home, where he provided what must surely have been the only mental companionship the priest then had.

Smoky had become poor. A severe illness had made it impossible for him to keep up his practice at the bar, though he still went daily to the Temple, which he could not bear to give up. He had become dependent on his wife—happily a rich woman then; but though no one could have treated the situation with more tact and delicacy than she did, it was bitterly galling to Smoky himself, who was now to some extent an invalid and could never hope to remedy it.

I did not confide my doubts or my search for some form of Christianity other than Catholicism to any of the few Catholics I still knew, neither did I confide in Smoky. The reason for this was that whilst I was trying to get out of the Church, he was trying to get into it. I knew that he had always wanted to be a Catholic and that it would be a real grief to him if he knew that I questioned my faith, still more if he knew that I no longer practised it. So for the first time in my life I used the policy—or, if you like, the deceit—of "non-disclosure" with Smoky.

He failed to get into the Church, and I failed to get out.

It was at this time increasingly obvious, both to me and to my mother, that I must soon make some attempt to earn my living. This necessity and my "search for Christianity" as I conceived it filled my whole mind.

For some time I had been attending an art school, though I never had the least wish to be a painter—indeed, the *only* thing I wanted to do was to write poetry, which was considered, rightly, a most unpromising means of livelihood. I had got, I think by a fluke, a scholarship to an art school, and at that my mother imagined (wrongly) that I had talent, and very over-optimistically entertained the hope that I would make a fortune as a commercial artist. I was persuaded to go in for the scholarship by an eccentric old Bohemian painter whom I chanced to meet at that time and who took a fancy to me. He insisted that I had great gifts for art, although I miserably insisted that I had none, nor even the inclination for it. However, he won the day and I won the scholarship, whereupon he agreed to teach me to paint himself, if I would learn to draw at the art school.

I was glad enough of this arrangement because it took me out of my home; the time I did not spend in the school I spent either in my old friend's studio or going with him in the evenings to the little affected, arty night-clubs that were springing up here and there in Soho. But I found time to go to one minister of religion after another to ask them to instruct me in their beliefs, which they did, and to attend every kind of religious service I could find. In these circumstances I naturally made a totally new set of friends, friends who could not have contrasted more strongly than they did with my former Catholic ones.

In the art school there were all the conventional unconventionals—long-haired men, short-haired women, both at that time considered to be shocking and delighting in it. They were all interested in ideas more than in things, and most of them were kind, provided that they were not asked to be kind to someone who was obviously not one of themselves. Then they were like wild birds pecking a caged one to death.

(At that time I held the false belief which so many young people hold—and even some foolish old ones—that the more immoral someone is, the kinder he is. I have discovered by experience that this is completely untrue. Nearly everyone is kind to those of his own convention; it takes a Christian to be kind to every sort of person, in every kind of circumstance, and not every Christian manages it.)

In my old painter's studio I met only very Bohemian and very eccentric people, and he was the most eccentric of them all. Approaching eighty years old, he was a great giant of a man, with a shock of thick white hair, stooping shoulders and piercing, cold blue eyes. He invariably went out in the streets wearing a bowler hat and, even on hot sunny days, the dirtiest mackintosh I have ever seen; strangest of all, he wore a pair of pink satin, high-heeled, woman's bedroom slippers—or, I suppose, bedroom boots—but how he ever came by them was a mystery to all his friends, as no one could imagine a woman with feet his size. In the streets little boys ran after him and mocked him, and it was my job to run behind him like a terrier and shoo them off. Happily he was deaf and heard only a very few of the mockeries. When he *did* hear, his rage was terrifying.

On the days that I spent painting in his studio he supplied me with food, but it was nauseating food—a bowl of raisins and some sickly, watered-down wine; this was his own staple diet, and he insisted that I share it—indeed, anyone who came was welcome to share it too, but few wanted to. He had no blankets or sheets on his bed, but simply covered himself at night with rugs from the floor, and I suspect that he slept at night in his mackintosh. Anyway, he was found dead on his bed one morning wearing it.

My old master's religion was art, nothing else at all but that; and to that he was wholly given. Everything that anyone did was justified if it were done in the cause of art. We painted from morning till night, stopping only when it was too dark to see, for he was too poor to use any form of artificial light, even candles. When it was really dark we normally went out to the clubs, or to someone else's studio.

He lived in a little colony of artists, and I made friends with those in the other studios as well as the students in the art school. I was happy in this environment, and these people were far more congenial to me than the respectable Catholics I had known before. I suppose that most of them were really hungering for some solid faith, just as I was myself, because there was constant talk of religion and spiritual things. Discussions and exchange of ideas would go on late into the night, and if anyone could afford a lamp we would gather round it and talk for hours. Most of these artists and students professed that curious thing called "my own religion," which usually in practice was *no* religion, and tended, as indeed my "own" religion did at that time, to recognise *only aesthetic,* not moral, values, and all manner of inconsistencies, provided they were prefixed by the word "free"—"free love," "free thought" and so on.

However, I did not confine myself to these discussions, interesting though they were. I wanted something more definite; I think that the buried insecurity of having been, for so long in my early childhood, the homeless child of a broken marriage made me feel my want of religious security acutely. At the same time I was not willing to accept it at the cost of personal dishonesty or even compromise. After all, I argued with myself, I knew nothing of the beliefs, or even the unbeliefs, of other people, and until I *did,* how could I form an honest opinion myself?

So I went to one clergyman after another, and one after the other received me with great kindness and gave me such instructions as they could in their different creeds. I say, "such as they could," because the instructions I received were astonishingly vague, and equally diverse. I began with the High Church, and descended gradually to Evangelical, to Low Church, and to Nonconformist. I went to the services too, and was often ashamed by the readiness of my emotional reactions to them. I preferred the Low Church services because the congregation put so much feeling into the hymn singing.

It did not seem to matter so much what you *believed,* so long as you *felt* good, and there was a certain amount of relief from nervous tension in this. The very High Church, on the other hand, seemed to me to be too much concerned about doctrine. No two clergymen— and I went to many High Church ones—seemed to believe quite the same, especially concerning such vital things as transubstantiation, and each one seemed to be trying to arrive at belief in some *one* particular doctrine through his own religion, not—as I knew a Catholic must (because Smoky had told me so)—to "swallow the lot whole, on the word of Jesus Christ."

In the Wesleyan chapels I experienced real emotional delight, it was like having warm water poured over you; and in the Salvation Army meetings I had to hold on to the bench to prevent myself from being swept forward on a wave of hysteria to "testify," even if this would involve inventing sins to confess in public which would come up to the Salvation Army standard of damnation and salvation.

When I had gone as far as I could in exploring the possible openings in Christianity, I turned to the Buddhists and the Jews. One of the artists living side by side with the old painter who befriended me was a Burmese half-caste, a Buddhist. He was not a great example of Eastern asceticism; indeed he was exceedingly lazy and sensual. At the same time he was a poet, and he would talk to me for hours about the beauty— at all events in theory—of his faith. He and his thirteen brothers had bought a peal of fourteen golden bells, one named after each of them, which they had hung up in the Burmese jungle, so that when the wind stirred them they would ring out prayers for their mother. He was also very fond of prayer wheels, which can be turned automatically and cut the effort out of prayer. Knowing him to be the laziest man in the world, I was not at all shocked by this idea of praying; after all, it showed the direction of his will, and it seemed to me very little different to a busy Catholic putting up a candle—with just this exception, that fire and light is a more beautiful symbol of prayer than a turning wheel, but not more beautiful than golden bells rocked by the wind, ringing out a prayer in the jungle that only God and the wild beasts could hear.

Most of the cleverest students in the art school were Jewish, and through one of them I was able to contact a rabbi—one whom she had in her family. He had very little use for me, though he was most courteous and gave me several instructions in the Jewish faith; and I went to the synagogue many times with his niece. It was in the synagogue that I became more and more convinced that I was running away from the thing I really wanted—the Catholic faith. There was something fierce and terrible, in a way, about the Jewish liturgy, but something familiar too. Deny it as I would, I could not help being more and more convinced that Christ was a seed that was sown in Israel to flower in the Catholic Church. However, after all these services and all these instructions I was no nearer to what I was seeking. Every creed that I was taught had *something* in it of truth and beauty, but it was always something that, even with my imperfect knowledge, I knew was included in the Catholic Church. Did the Catholic Church include everything? This was the question which began to puzzle and trouble me more and more, for, frankly, I did not *want* to be a Catholic.

What I did want, and with increasing longing, was to join the Russian Church. By this time I had many Russian friends, and both those who practised their religion and those who did not seemed to me more deeply and sincerely Christian than any other people I had ever met. Compared to the far colder people of the Western forms of Christianity, they would indeed have seemed to be illogical and inconsistent, but to me the reverse seemed to be the case. Most of the Russians were ready to tolerate everything, unready to judge anything. They knew themselves to be sinners, and indeed took it for granted quite happily that we are all sinners, and in spite of the arrogance inherent in the character of the Russian aristocracy they had always a profound humility. Their charity was boundless, and their realisation of the closeness and the love of Christ, here and now in this world, an almost tangible thing. They were always extreme, but their extremes seemed to me so much more lovable, even when they were outrageous, than what I considered the watered-down religious passions and the mediocrities of the West.

For example, I thought that Russian Christians were often despots, but never, like Western Christians, petty snobs. A Russian might beat you, he might even stab you, but he would never cut you dead in the street because he did not consider you to be respectable. Again, they had the ideal of the "humiliated Christ." They did not, as we do, think of Christ as a *perfect* man in body as well as in soul, and cherished a legend of Him being lame and limping through Russia from time to time all through history, begging His way. All this went straight home to me, and so too did the beauty of the Russian liturgy, which is to my taste incomparably more beautiful than ours. At the time I was unaware of the existence of the agelong *Catholic* Russian liturgy, which is now my greatest consolation.

But I could not join the Russian Church: I enquired tentatively of Smoky about the schism between East and West, and his answers in favour of the West—and of the Pope—seemed indisputable. Moreover, I learnt from my friends that the Russians were to some extent identifying themselves with the Anglo-Catholics, and this seemed to me an absolute barrier.

No, I seemed to be homeless spiritually, as I had been materially as a child, and I lived perilously; cut off from the sacraments by my own action, possessing now a merely aesthetic conscience, inflated by the conceit of youth, I was a ready victim to every temptation. However, I was suddenly obliged to earn my bread, and so, flung out of myself and into many more contacts with other people.

Chapter 12

One morning, for reasons that need not be told here, I decided to leave home and make myself independent. I did so, and took a room in a lodging-house, though I did not know how I would pay the rent. I told this frankly to the landlady and, knowing it, she took me in. My room was cheap because, owing to a broken chimney, it was impossible to have a fire in it. However, that did not worry me; all I wanted was a roof over my head and a table to sit and write at. There was, however, very little chance to sit and write, as I had to set about earning my living.

I had no qualifications of any sort. So far as painting and drawing were concerned, I could do only the most impractical work. Encouraged by my own painting master, who was now dead, I had completely ignored commercial art. I was illiterate, in the sense that I could not spell or punctuate. Although I had done a great deal of housework at home, I was very inefficient even in that, and, further, lacked the physical stamina to do it well.

However, I managed to get a series of most varied jobs. One was in commercial art. The office I worked in was in Ludgate Hill; my lodging, in St. John's Wood. My pay was 15/- a week (in those days 15/- equalled about 25/- today); I was obliged to walk to and from the office and to go without lunch, but I hoped that I was getting "experience" which would lead to better work. Every agency I had been to had told me that without "experience" there was no hope, but how to get this precious thing before you start is a problem which I have still not solved.

I remember one day asking an old man outside St. Paul's Cathedral, where I spent my hungry lunch hour, to give me a piece of the bread with which he was feeding the pigeons. He refused, because, he said, he loved birds, not people! This answer puzzled me. My own attitude to people had radically changed since I had seen the "Russian icon," and since the necessity of earning my living had forced me to go out and meet all kinds of people. I was still tormented by morbid shyness and a distressing consciousness of being "peculiar" myself, but in spite of that, people—those I knew *and* those I did not know—fascinated me in an extraordinary, even an obsessive way. I felt that somehow, in some way not yet clear to me, there must be a kind of mystical relationship between people, a bond which was wholly independent of exterior things; a kind of relationship which enabled all to help all, even though they were not acquainted. This, like so much else in my life, came to me through odd flashes and intuitions. It was not a thought-out thing at all.

My room was at the top of the house. The sounds that came up from the street were quite unlike sounds that one hears on the street level; down there they fill the ears, but far above, they seem to be in some curious way filtered, and to go in essence to the mind. I think the fact that I was usually hungry made me very much more sensitive to sounds and their significance than I would have been otherwise. Despite my wish to sit at my table and write, I was seldom able to. When I got back to my lodging, I was cold and hungry and tired; I had walked to and from the City, and I wanted to sit in the dark and listen.

Every night at about ten o'clock, when I was sitting huddled on my bed in the dark, I heard the tap, tap, tap of a blind man's stick, passing below in the street. It had an extraordinary effect on me. Somehow, between me and this unknown blind man there was an affinity. Was I not spiritually blind? Was I not, too, tapping, here, there and everywhere, longing for light, but feeling my way in darkness, because the darkness was not in the night that was lit by the splendour of the stars, but in my own soul? I began to pray for this blind man—and I had almost lost the habit of prayer.

I began, too, to feel an urge to go out and walk about at night among the London crowds. Until now my interest had been in two sorts of people—those whom I actually knew personally, and the far-off Russians, of whom I was always conscious, as people living through the Passion in our own days. Now—curious as it may seem—because of this blind man, whom I had never seen, tapping with his stick in the night, I wanted to go out and rub shoulders with the London crowds. In some sort of way, which I could not yet define, I wanted to *take part* in these countless lives that I began to realise as pressing on me.

As it happened, I was forced out. Exhausted or not, I found my 15/- a week insufficient for my rent, such light as I used, the few necessary clothes and the one very small meal a day to which I limited myself. Consequently I did go out, and during the first year or two after I left home did a most extraordinarily varied number of jobs.

The firm where I worked as a commercial artist was short-lived; before the end my employer paid me in chocolates instead of shillings, and I had to give the chocolates away, as they are not easily digested on an empty stomach. It became imperative to take evening work, and so I returned to the little arty clubs that I had frequented in my old painting master's days, and offered myself as a letter-writer. I could not spell the letters correctly, but I assured my customers that there was no letter I could not compose, from the most moving love letter to the most vindictive utterance of hate. Most of my customers wanted love letters, and sometimes I had as many as ten or twelve a night to write, at a shilling each.

I had many other jobs by day; one, to look after ten children in a boarding house, while their mothers, all either widowed or divorced, went out in search of new husbands. Again, I joined a troupe of actors—which, of course, interfered with my night-club work, as we toured the outskirts of London and performed by night in third-rate halls. I had *no* histrionic talent, but none was required of me. I did not have to appear at all, but only to play the part of "noises off" from the wings. I had two roles: "Sound of a cock crowing" and "Sound of husband and wife quarrelling." The latter was by far more difficult.

I varied these jobs by becoming alternately an interior decorator and a charwoman. Both were a financial failure: the interior decorating because my patrons, though delighted by the results, seldom paid me, and I was incapable of reminding them of their debt; the cleaning because, owing to an ungovernable terror of mice, dead or alive, which has obsessed my life, I could not bring myself to remove dead ones from traps in the kitchens where I worked, and was obliged to bribe the cooks with nearly all my wages to do it for me. My wages were very small and the bribes were demanded every day.

All this necessity to work was good for me. It forced me to make innumerable and most varied contacts, and I became more and more interested in other people as well as—and I sincerely believe even more than—in myself. Whenever I was able to do so, usually on Sunday nights, I walked about among the crowds. My favourite beat was the Edgware Road, a very sordid road; I had the impression that in spite of that, here everyone was intensely alive.

It had another advantage for me; the various third-rate eating-shops and fish-and-chip bars stank. People have told me that they have stood in front of such with their mouths watering. It was not so with me; I had only to stand in front of one for a few minutes to feel not only fed but surfeited—not only surfeited but disgusted, and so prevented from the smallest desire for food.

From the Edgware Road I came to Hyde Park—and in Hyde Park discovered the Catholic Evidence Guild. It became my only link with the Church; and it became a very strong one. This, it seemed to me, was *really* Christianity and Catholicism as one thing. At first I was in doubt; I thought that perhaps this was yet another religion, a kind of crank religion founded by the young speaker who I now know was Frank Sheed. But gradually I realized that it was nothing of the sort. It was the Catholic Church—but it was the Catholic

Church being Christ; not waiting for the people to come in, but coming out to the people. It was *really*, in a way that I could not understand, Christ following His lost sheep—of whom I was one.

Chapter 13

Perhaps what I have written will give the impression to those who have never lived from hand to mouth (especially when the hand occasionally fails to reach the mouth) that my time of poverty was also a time of misery. It was far from it. Had I wanted to, I could have made an end of it at any moment; I had not been turned out of my home—I had walked out of my own accord, and I had not walked far, for my lodging was in the same street as the house I had left. I need never have been hungry, for without going home again to live, I could have gone home to eat. But I very seldom did. With curious presumption, I was confident that God, whom I was forsaking, would not forsake me; I was too certain that He would give me all that I really needed, to feel the least anxiety about the next meal or the next week's rent, and in this I was right—there was always just enough, and it was always just in time.

Very soon the lodging-house that I was living in was filled by fellow students and fellow workers of mine, and I wanted to live as they did, as one of them. We shared the same uncertainty, but we shared everything else too—not by agreement, but spontaneously, as something taken for granted.

In those days that dreadful description, "a displaced person," was unknown, but I was one, spiritually and mentally, by my own choosing. I had separated myself from the Church to which I belonged, from the family of the faithful, and from my own little family. I was lonely, in spite of my good friends, but I knew instinctively that mine was a curious kind of loneliness which could never be ended even by the closest relationship with individuals, but only, in some mysterious way which I could not yet understand, by some kind of communion with all men, everywhere in the world. I was driven by a powerful compulsion even to pursue this loneliness, and precisely because it was in the London streets that I was most aware of it, I often walked about among the crowds for hours. I had gradually ceased to look for Christ in the churches and had begun, though I had not yet realised it, to look for Him in the streets and in the people who thronged them.

Nevertheless, I longed for the Blessed Sacrament and

the beauty of the liturgy of the Church, and this longing was made bitter to me by the perverse idea I had fostered, that the Blessed Sacrament had been put out of my reach because it had been put into the hands of the hard and righteous people in whom I felt I could have no part. It did not dawn on me that in condemning others wholesale as Pharisees, I myself was a Pharisee. Had anyone suggested this to me, I would have been dumbfounded, for I prided myself on condoning the sins of the most disreputable people—people who, I am certain, were far less guilty for their sins than I was for mine, since many of them had grown up without any knowledge of God. Without knowing it, I was being patronising as well as Pharisaical.

By depriving myself of the beauty of the Church's liturgy, as well as of her sacraments, I was driving myself to a dangerous state of psychological, as well as spiritual, starvation, and becoming more and more driven by my own emotions. I had emptied myself of almost everything that was essential to me, and now felt the necessity of filling that emptiness. I did not define *this*, but obviously it added a fierce intensity to every natural temptation and complicated all my emotional relationships with other people. In spite of my infidelity I still regarded myself as a Catholic and still regarded my sins as being sins. I had not yet completely thrown off what I thought of as "the yoke" of Catholicism; consequently, though I did many things that I knew to be wrong, I still resisted any action that would put me definitely "out of the Church" for good.

Now I was tempted to do that; to turn my back on the Church once and for all, and to take what happiness life seemed to offer me outside it. I argued that since I was incapable of arriving at absolute truth by my own seeking, I might as well give up seeking; that as I was incapable of being happy in the Church, I might as well be as happy as I could outside. But all these arguments were so many sops to my conscience; the simple truth was that I was being swept by temptation as dry grass is swept by a flame of fire.

Then, for the third time, I "saw" Christ in man.

This time it was an unimaginably vaster experience than on either of the other occasions; it was not a seeing of Christ in one person, as it had been with the Bavarian nun, or in one particular sort of person, as it had been in the living icon of Christ the King. This time it was Christ in all men. This is much more difficult to describe than the other experiences; I can only do my best to tell it just as it happened.

I was in an underground train, a crowded train in which all sorts of people jostled together, sitting and strap-hanging—workers of every description going home at the end of the day. Quite suddenly I saw with my mind, but as vividly as a wonderful picture, Christ in them all. But I saw more than that; not only was Christ in every one of them, living in them, dying in them, rejoicing in them, sorrowing in them—but because He was in them, and because they were here, the whole world was here too, here in this underground train; not only the world as it was at that moment, not only all the people in all the countries of the world, but all those people who had lived in the past, and all those yet to come.

I came out into the street and walked for a long time in the crowds. It was the same here, on every side, in every passer-by, everywhere—Christ.

I had long been haunted by the Russian conception of the humiliated Christ, the lame Christ limping through Russia, begging His bread; the Christ who, all through the ages, might return to the earth and come even to sinners to win their compassion by His need. Now, in the flash of a second, I knew that this dream is a fact; not a dream, not the fantasy or legend of a devout people, not the prerogative of the Russians, but Christ in man. It belongs therefore to the Catholic Church; Christ in His perfect human nature, Christ in His risen glory *and* Christ in His need and His suffering on earth, are reconciled. We have the whole Christ.

The "vision" lasted with that intensity for several days, and each of them revealed the mystery and its implications for me a little more clearly. Although it did not prevent me from ever sinning again, it showed me what sin is, especially those sins done in the name of "love," so often held to be "harmless"—for to sin with one whom you loved was to blaspheme Christ in that person; it was to spit on Him, perhaps to crucify Him. I saw too the reverence that everyone must have for a sinner; instead of condoning his sin, which is in reality his utmost sorrow, one must comfort Christ who is suffering in him. And this reverence must be paid even to those sinners whose souls seem to be dead, because it is Christ, who is the life of the soul, who is dead in them; they are His tombs, and Christ in the tomb is potentially the risen Christ. For the same reason, no one of us who has fallen into mortal sin himself must ever lose hope.

It would be impossible to set down here all the implications of this "vision" of Christ in man; it altered the course of my life completely, and in a sense took away my difficulty about the Blessed Sacrament's being put into the hands of sinners. I saw that it is the will of Christ's love *to* be put into the hands of sinners, to trust Himself to men, that He may be *their* gift to one another, that *they* may comfort Him in each other, give Him to each other. In this sense the ordinary life itself becomes sacramental, and every action of anyone at all has an eternal meaning.

I knew too that since Christ is One in all men, as He is One in countless Hosts, everyone is included in Him; there can be no outcasts, no excommunicates, excepting those who excommunicate themselves—and they too may be saved, Christ rising from death in them.

Christ is everywhere; in Him every kind of life has a meaning and has an influence on every other kind of life. It is not the foolish sinner like myself, running about the world with reprobates and feeling magnanimous, who comes closest to them and brings them healing; it is the contemplative in her cell who has never set eyes on them, but in whom Christ fasts and prays for them—or it may be a charwoman in whom Christ makes

Himself a servant again, or a king whose crown of gold hides a crown of thorns. Realization of our oneness in Christ is the only cure for human loneliness. For me, too, it is the only ultimate meaning of life, the only thing that gives meaning and purpose to every life.

After a few days the "vision" faded. People looked the same again, there was no longer the same shock of insight for me each time I was face to face with another human being. Christ was hidden again; indeed, through the years to come I would have to seek for Him, and usually I would find Him in others—and still more in myself— only through a deliberate and blind act of faith. But if the "vision" had faded, the knowledge had not; on the contrary, that knowledge, touched by a ray of the Holy Spirit, is like a tree touched by the sun—it puts out leaf and flowers, bearing fruit and blossom from splendour to splendour.

For me, the greatest joy in being once again in full communion with the Catholic Church has been, and is now, the ever-growing reassurance given by the doctrine of the Mystical Body of Christ, with its teaching that *we* are the Church, and that "Christ and His Church are one"—and that *because* Christ and His Church are one, the world's sorrow, with which I have always been obsessed, and which is a common obsession in these tragic years, is only the shadow cast by the spread arms of the crucified King to shelter us until the morning of resurrection from the blaze of everlasting love.